NOEL PURCELL

George Formby: a Catalogue of His Work

Jimmy O'Dea, the Pride of the Coombe

Noel PURCELL

a biography

PHILIP B RYAN

POOLBEG

First published 1992 by
Poolbeg Press Ltd
Knocksedan House,
Swords, Co Dublin, Ireland

© Philip B Ryan, 1992

The moral right of the author has been asserted.

Poolbeg Press receives assistance from
the Arts Council / An Chomhairle Ealaíon, Ireland.

ISBN 1 85371 197 7

A catalogue record for this book is available from the British Library

Cover design by Pomphrey Associates
Cover still from the Metro-Goldwyn-Mayer film, *Lust for Life*
Set by Richard Parfrey in ITC Stone Serif 9.5/15
Linotronic output by Seton Music Graphics, Bantry
Printed by Colour Books, Baldoyle

For
Eileen Purcell

CONTENTS

FOREWORD

Many years ago, as a young schoolboy at Marian College in Sandymount, I, along with every other boy in the class, gazed in awe at the long fin-backed American Pontiac that often swept around Lansdowne Road and into Newbridge Avenue, where Noel Purcell then lived. He was our first movie-star and was at that time the only movie-star living in Dublin. Of course, there were Barry Fitzgerald, Maureen O'Hara and Arthur Shields, but they did not *live* here, or at least we never saw them about the place. Noel Purcell looked like a cross between Moses and Santa Claus.

Noel Purcell was the definitive Dubliner. When we were children his voice was a fixture on the Walton's sponsored programme on Radio Éireann. (Remember "If you feel like singing, do sing an Irish song"?) The Dubliners and other Irish folk groups made Noel's song "The Dublin Saunter" (or "Dublin Can Be Heaven," as they called it) their party piece, especially when they were away from home.

Many years later I met him to discuss the possibility of his returning to the stage. He made his first comeback to the stage of the Gaiety with *You Ain't Heard Nuthin' Yet*. He was seventy-eight years old and he was sensational. He and Cecil Sheridan appeared in one scene seated on a park bench. They sang a duet by Kurt Weill called "September Song" and it brought the house down every night. The following year, Noel played Jacob in the revival of *Joseph and His Amazing Technicolor Dreamcoat*.

Working with Noel was for me more than the realisation of a schoolboy dream. His stagecraft was extraordinary and he had instant rapport with his audience. Despite his vast experience of sixty years on stage and in films he was never patronising to any of the younger actors or singers. In fact he was extremely helpful and always good-humoured.

Many a night after the show, we younguns would sit in the Circle Bar listening to Noel's fascinating stories about Hollywood, the Theatre Royal, the Gaiety and all the people he had known—"Mr Louis" (Louis Elliman), James Mason, Gregory Peck, Marlon Brando, Richard Harris, James Cagney, Rock Hudson, Peter O'Toole and many more, including his pals from the Dublin theatre like Eddie Byrne, Josef Locke and Dick Forbes.

I think he was the one Dubliner who could have walkéd an open election for Lord Mayor of the city, if he had wanted it. He was, however, bigger than the Lord Mayor; he was the Dubs' Dub.

The author, Philip B Ryan, is to be complimented on the fine research and the obvious hard work which he has put into this biography.

Noel Pearson
April 1992

PREFACE

From the very beginnings of Music Hall, all of the great stars had at least one song with which they were immediately identified. The first was probably George Leybourne with his "Champagne Charlie" and others of that era were Marie Lloyd and her "Oh! Mr Porter" and Charles Coburn and "The Man Who Broke the Bank at Monte Carlo." Harry Lauder was forever "Roamin' in the Gloamin'." George Formby Senior with "John Willie, Come On!" was succeeded years later by his son, George Formby Junior who knew all about the exploits of "The Window Cleaner" when he wasn't "Leaning on a Lamp Post" and, of course, Flanagan and Allen lived "Underneath the Arches." The list is endless, but it must include Jimmy O'Dea and his "Biddy Mulligan the Pride of the Coombe." Another Irish performer, one who memorably sang about the delights of Dublin on a sunny summer morning, was Noel Purcell who sang his "Dublin Saunter" in much better voice and in a style reminiscent of the elegant Jack Buchanan.

In January 1981, towards the end of Noel's stage career, RTE Television produced a programme about the old Dublin Liberties area starring a young Liberties lad and rising star, Tony Kenny. Tony took viewers on a conducted tour of this ancient part of Dublin with nostalgic reminders of people and places long since gone and enlivened the experience by interpolating some appropriate songs. Tony strolled leisurely on his way towards St Patrick's Park, green and sun-drenched, singing "The Dublin Saunter" to the accompaniment of an invisible orchestra.

I've been north and I've been south and I've been east and west,
I've been just a rolling stone.
Yet there's one place on this earth I've always liked the best
Just a little town I call my own.

Chorus
Dublin can be heaven with coffee at eleven, and a stroll in
    Stephen's Green;
There's no need to hurry, there's no need to worry: you're a
    king and the lady's a queen.
Grafton Street's a wonderland, there's magic in the air;
There are diamonds in the lady's eyes and gold dust in her
    hair;
And if you don't believe me, come and meet me there,
In Dublin on a sunny summer morning.

I've been here and I've been there, I've sought the rainbow's
    end;
But no crock of gold I've found.
Now I know that come what will, whatever fate may send,
Here my roots are deep in friendly ground.

Chorus

This song summed up Noel Purcell and, to an even greater extent, his life. Here was the quintessential Dubliner, who revelled in the city and its people, all of whom he seemed to know personally as friends. During the course of years of global travel making countless films, he was always relieved to find himself back on the stages of his beloved Theatre Royal or Gaiety Theatre.

As Tony was finishing the song, the television camera caught in a long shot the figure of an old gentleman with a magnificent grey-white beard sitting alone on a park bench, hand at side of head as if listening intently and as they drew level in a close-up shot, the lone man turned to Tony and said:

"That's not a bad one son, where did you get that?"

The man was, of course, Noel Purcell himself, delighted, no doubt, that if he could no longer sing his song as he used to, it was being given new life by one of the newer, up-and-coming young fellows.

In the future, even as it is now, coffee at eleven in the wonderland of Grafton Street as you approach it from St Stephen's Green will be synonymous with Noel Purcell. He won't be there himself to greet you as "me ould brown son" and nobody else will dare act the impostor by borrowing the exclusive salutation, for this was Noel's personal greeting reserved for his best friends.

NOEL PURCELL

ACKNOWLEDGEMENTS

We are deeply indebted to Mrs Eileen Purcell whose gracious assistance made this book possible.

We are grateful to the following for their invaluable help:

Majella Breen, Sound Archives, RTE; musician-producer Kevin Byrne; Mary Clarke, Dublin City Archivist; author Séamus de Búrca; John Doyle, a habitué of the Theatre Royal; Barbara Durack, Programme Library, RTE; photographer Joe Dillon of Tuam; John Finegan, retired theatre correspondent of the *Evening Herald*; actor Séamus Forde; Tony Hannah, EMI Records; Joe Kearns, late retired director-manager of the Gaiety Theatre, Dublin; entertainer Tony Kenny; singer Seán Mooney; the Secretary, Synge Street CBS; and finally Sean McMahon, Jo O'Donoghue and Margaret Daly who were involved in the preparation and publicising of this book.

We sincerely regret the passing of Joe Kearns. During the research for this biography, Joe delighted in reminiscing about his old friend Noel Purcell. Happily, he saw a draft of the book before his death in May 1992.

We are indebted to the various film companies whose stills are reproduced in this book. Full details of the films and their producers appear in the Filmography. The front cover picture of Noel Purcell is from the Metro-Goldwyn-Mayer film *Lust for Life*. We have quoted briefly from published copyright material; all credits are given in the Bibliography.

We have been unable to trace Twinkle Forbes, who we believe to be the copyright owner of her father's monologues, "Spring," "Winter," and "The Man in the Street," which are reproduced in this book. The Harry O'Donovan sketch, "Would You Like to Take a Walk," is reproduced by kind permission of Terry O'Donovan. "But Now I Know" by Philip Green is copyright Photoplay Music Ltd, 9 Cavendish Square, London.

CHAPTER ONE

In November 1984, hotelier PV Doyle decided that his exclusive new Westbury Hotel hadn't been christened properly, so he decided to host a special luncheon for his life-long friend, Noel Purcell and forty of his other friends, a list which included Gay Byrne; Kathleen Watkins (who, being under the impression that the event was being held at the Berkeley Court Hotel, arrived thirty minutes late); Ted Nealon, Minister of State for the Arts, who talked of the Theatre Royal and admitted he used to watch the Royalettes instead of Noel; Dr Brendan Smith of the Olympia; Joe Kearns, Manager of the Gaiety; Gerry Harvey of An Post, whose father, the popular Jimmy Harvey, had appeared with Noel in the Queen's; horsy man GW Robinson; city manager Frank Feely; Rick and Ivy Bourke of the Variety Club; Gerry McGuinness; Brian McSharry; Leo Ward; Noel Mountaine; Oona McWhirter, late publicity director of the Royal; and many more.

Noel, who would be eighty-four in the following month, arrived in a wheelchair that was quickly abandoned. "It's a method of convenience," he explained. "The ould pins aren't what they used to be." Noel and his wife Eileen were greeted by Mr Doyle who recalled happy days in the Gaiety Theatre watching Noel on stage with Jimmy O'Dea. "Thank you Noel," he said, "for making Grafton Street a wonderland, and today, Noel, you are the king

and Eileen is the queen." Gay Byrne recalled that three years previously he and a few friends went along to the Adelaide Hospital on Christmas Eve: "Noel was in dry dock, although at the time we arrived he did not seem to be too dry." Gay added: "Now it's three years later and I feel worse than he looks now!" Apart from the fact that Mr Doyle planned the function to honour a very special friend, he was aware that Noel had in fact a tenuous connection in the past with the actual site upon which the hotel now stood. There had once been a kindergarten school in Clarendon Street and Noel learned his ABC there. The Westbury had been built through a winter and summer but PV Doyle felt it would never be finally launched until this day happened. "I wanted Noel here," he confessed. "Only then did I feel it would be properly christened."

The kindergarten school referred to was part of quite a large convent school run by the Holy Faith nuns. The top storey was a private school with eighteen or twenty boys who remained until they made their first communion. The nuns never referred to fees as such: they were known as the "pension" and Noel's mother paid a golden half-sovereign when it became due each term. The area around Clarendon Street was the heartland of Dublin in those days and the butcher and fish shops in Chatham Street were considered the best in the city. Over McDonagh's butcher's shop there was a very impressive shield which announced that the McDonaghs were "By Appointment to the Lord Lieutenant."

After kindergarten, Noel attended the Christian Brothers school at Synge Street where he claimed "I got the bejapers beaten out of me; I wasn't a brilliant scholar, I don't think." Two of Noel's fellow pupils at Synge Street were Paddy and Todd Andrews, the latter being the guiding light of Bord na Móna. Noel claimed that he and Todd were always relegated to the back bench in the classroom. He mentioned that other playmates were Seán and Noel Lemass but firm details of their youthful association are vague. Noel's sporting activities included rugby; his friend Paddy Andrews said that Noel played as a forward for CYMS but he was far better at acting than playing rugby. On one occasion Noel was running towards the line when a much smaller opponent rashly tackled the tall figure, only to be sent flying. Noel stopped short of the line, dropped the ball and went back down the field to help the lad to his feet and enquire, "Did I hurt you, friend?" Handball was the game of the era and the wall down at Ferrier Pollock's provided perfect height and surface.

Noel also appeared in amateur shows at the CYMS in Harrington Street, where the Garda Club is now. No girls were allowed in the CYMS so the boys played girls' roles. Noel was amused to recall fellows like Todd Andrews and all those other lads playing the parts of girls. This was a practice that survived until fairly recently all over Dublin in the Christian Brothers' productions of Gilbert and Sullivan operettas.

The Holy Faith nuns had instructed some of their pupils, including Noel, to serve as altar boys for the Carmelites in Clarendon Street church. It was there, as he admits, that he learned to smoke. He shared the Latin responses with boys like McMahon, who would later become a famous jockey, and the boy patriot, Kevin Barry, who, as an eighteen-year-old student and member of the IRA, was arrested and badly beaten up and tortured before being hanged in 1920. Noel remembered him as "a nice little fellow, a sweet young man, a year or so younger than me—his mother had a dairy in Fleet Street."

He was born Patrick Joseph Noel Purcell on 23 December 1900. Many reports describe him as an only child but he did in fact have a younger sister, who died of diphtheria when she was five. As a matter of passing interest, the pantomimes running in the Dublin theatres that Christmas were: *Little Red Riding Hood* at the Gaiety (a panto which would have great significance for Noel years later); *Robinson Crusoe* at the Theatre Royal (again a panto which would later serve to determine the direction of Noel's life), and *Blue Beard* at the Queen's Royal Theatre (a tenuous connection, really; in the future Noel's famous beard was always grey-white).

His mother, Catherine, whose maiden name was Hoban was a native of Dublin. Born on 2 October 1872, she was the owner of two houses in Lower Mercer Street: 11a where Noel was born and the property next door No 12, in which her sister lived. Catherine was a familiar figure in the area because of her antique business which she operated from the ground floor of 11A. She was an acknowledged expert in the trade which she probably inherited from her family and many dealers of repute came to her for her opinions and advice. She specialised particularly in Dresden china and other such lovely examples of perfect craftsmanship. She numbered among her customers the curator of the National Museum and the two Archbishops of Dublin. Another frequent browser was Jim Hicks of Pembroke Street whose hand-carpentered furniture is a proud possession today for anyone lucky enough to own a piece. Hicks also constructed and furnished what was known as "The Queen's Dolls House" and Tommy Lennon travelled the world assembling it for public display. It had a miniature Steinway piano which would be played by stroking the notes with a pin. "I met them all," said Noel. "They'd come in and have a cup of tea with my mother in the back kitchen. They'd talk about Baxter prints and different painters and paintings. But I remember the Baxter prints because they were often used to illustrate the front covers of sheet music. What a pity I didn't listen to the conversations between the clients and my mother—I would have learned something."

It is probable that Noel's mother met her husband in the course of her business transactions, as Pierce Purcell was an auctioneer with Lawlor Briscoe (this would have been the father of Robert Briscoe, the first Jewish Lord Mayor of Dublin) of Lower Ormond Quay. Purcell was a native of Thurles, Co Tipperary. The name Purcell is from the French—*pourcel* (little pig). This Anglo-Norman family was one of those which became completely Hibernicised.

They distinguished themselves in the wars of the seventeenth century and were numbered later among the "Wild Geese." Captain James Purcell and Colonel Nicholas Purcell, powerful landowners, were brothers in arms of Patrick Sarsfield, and Nicholas Purcell was one of the signatories of the Treaty of Limerick in 1691. They were settled mainly in Tipperary. Noel's boyhood was a strange mixture of the religious ritual of the altar boy, a love of sport and a pleasure in the rough and tumble of the streets which were cobblestoned and gave a peculiarly sensuous pleasure when they were walked upon in bare feet. (The love of ritual was to remain with him to a great degree. In later years he often found himself serving Mass for some forgotten priest in Fiji or Tahiti when he was filming there, but he could never get really accustomed to the new English rite.) Noel recalled, "The local hardchaws used to take their shoes off and I thought it was great to take mine off too, but my mother took a dim view because when I'd walk back into the shop, you never knew who you might find there, perhaps the Catholic Archbishop of Dublin, Dr Walsh." Later, when he became a star at the Theatre Royal, his script-writer Dick Forbes wrote a line into a monologue about "Conn of the Hundred Fights," a figure from Irish history: "For I was born in Mercer Street where the kids play tag with hatchets."

But the days of stardom were in the far distance. Noel's mother had a friend named Martin Murphy, a man of independent mind, who doubled as stage-manager and stage carpenter at the Gaiety Theatre and one day he asked Noel if he would like to go to the theatre to see the show. Murphy brought Noel thirty feet up to the flies where George Morrison soon taught him how to pulley-haul and fly the scenery and borders. Sometimes he stood down in the wings at the side of the stage where he could watch everything as if he were on the stage himself with the performers. One day the call-boy was fired and Murphy suggested to young Noel, then aged twelve, that as he was in the theatre most evenings anyhow, he might as well take the job. He was instructed to go round the dressing rooms and call the half hour, quarter hour and finally overture and beginners. He was given a half sovereign in wages at the end of the first week, because it was his first week, but thereafter he was given the regular rate of a shilling a night which meant that with six shows a week and a matinée on Saturday, he was in receipt of seven shillings a week. And so began his career in the theatre.

The stage hands at that time were part-timers getting one shilling and sixpence a show; they were mainly civil servants doing a bit of moonlighting. Noel's mother didn't object to his activities and regarded them as an improvement on playing in the streets but she did insist on his staying on at school until he was sixteen. She had hopes of his becoming a doctor but Noel didn't have the urge for too much studying and, besides, he was happy to attend school by day and spend his evenings in the Gaiety. One of his earliest memories was of the first appearance there of the new amateur group, the Rathmines and Rathgar Musical Society, who presented *The Mikado* in December 1913. They had already done a show in the Queen's but they were very inexperienced and nervous, so Noel and the stage hands, Buck Algar, "Sloppy" McGuinness and Billy Amery, the prop man, helped out by joining in the choruses off-stage. "We sounded louder than the chorus," said Noel.

Very soon the new call-boy received an unexpected bit of promotion: a Scottish company called The Moffats were doing a play called *Bunty Pulls the Strings* with Cyril Maude and Noel was given a walk-on part as a messenger boy who upon being offered a penny replies in his best Scottish accent, "I'd rather have a packet of Woodbines." Noel recalled that he never rehearsed anything like he rehearsed that line. Later, in 1914, he got a walk-on part as the little middy in the D'Oyly Carte production of *HMS Pinafore*. A walk-on was worth sixpence a night. (He was unlucky in the following year as he had grown so tall that they couldn't fit him into the uniform. When Noel was sixteen he was over six foot tall and still growing.) Later that year he and another lad, Buck Colgan, got one supporting role between them as a donkey in a fantastic play called *The Brass Bottle*, in which Noel was the hind legs; a circumstance which gave rise to his claim ever afterwards that he started his acting career "from the bottom up."

There was a long bench outside the number-one dressing room at the Gaiety and Noel would sit on it during the long evenings being helped with his homework by the great visiting stars of the day. Soon he was given more responsibility, helping the stage electrician, Harry Morrison, to work the ancient lighting system. The dimmers were like great sewer pipes about six foot long filled up with ammonium chloride and the electrical lines were lowered into the fluid and that dimmed the lights. One night they went wrong and Harry Morrison got stuck on them and the fellow that went to get him off found himself stuck also because Harry was live—the whole lot had to be taken down to get them off it. Fire was a constant terror but in all his days in the Dublin theatres, Noel never experienced a fire in which life was lost. He attributed this to a man called Stephen Stapleton who was the *bête noire* of Dublin theatre managers. He had only to be seen approaching a theatre and the word went round: "Stapleton's in! Look out!" Stapleton was a corporation fire officer and a martinet; there was no arguing with him. He'd say, "You tell your light board that I want a new three-inch teak door on that," and a new three-inch teak door would appear overnight.

From his lighting perch high up on the proscenium arch, the "lime boy", Noel Purcell, nightly shone his spotlight on some of the greatest actors the theatre has ever seen: Sir John Martin Harvey; Gerald du Maurier; Sir Seymour Hicks; Sir Frank Benson; Fred and Julia Terry; Fanny Moody; Mrs Patrick Campbell; Ouida McDermott and many more. But there can be absolutely no doubt that the greatest influence on the impressionable young man was made by the visiting opera companies like Carl Rosa, the O'Meara Opera Company and the Moody Manners Company. He developed an abiding love of opera and indeed to the end of his long life he could quote many of them from memory.

Occasionally, Martin Murphy would send Noel to a little theatre in O'Connell Street to help out with the scenery changes. This was Madame Rocke's Theatre, opposite the Gresham Hotel and was housed over Cramer Woods piano shop. It held about fifty people and was furnished with proper tip-up seats. There Noel met Thomas MacDonagh, the revolutionary, and his brother John, who later wrote revues for Jimmy O'Dea. The Countess Markievicz and Joseph Plunkett were also frequent visitors. Noel claimed that he never saw Pádraig Pearse—"He was a foreigner," said Noel, "living out in Rathfarnham!"

Now approaching the age of fifteen, Noel was offered a role with Edward Martyn's Irish Players in a hall in Hardwicke Street which also housed the Dun Emer Guild, which dealt in hand-loom tapestries and hand-printed books. The Irish Players specialised principally in foreign plays as a contrast to the Irish plays at the Abbey, and Noel's future colleague, Jimmy O'Dea, scored one of his first early successes there in the role of Firs in Chekhov's *The Cherry Orchard*. Noel played the role of the young Doolan in an unusual play, *A Phoenix on the Roof*, by the Irish writer, Eimar O'Duffy. He has stated that he appeared in this play in Madame Rocke's theatre but in this he must have had a lapse of memory, as scholarly research indicates that the play was presented in the 1914–5 season at the Hardwicke Hall. He received a fee of one shilling and sixpence a night but this handsome increase from his shilling a night at the Gaiety was diminished somewhat by travelling expenses, the tram fare to Hardwicke Street being a penny. It is probable that Noel was able to accept this engagement only because films had been introduced temporarily at the Gaiety. The existing picture houses were too small to accommodate DW Griffith's film masterpiece *The Birth of a Nation* so it was first screened at the Gaiety where it ran for twenty-four performances and had to be revived shortly afterwards with an additional twelve showings.

Noel remembered his role as Doolan as not much more than a walk-on part, but the theatre historian Joseph Holloway reported that the audience enjoyed the characterisation so much that O'Duffy may have built up the role in his revision. Holloway interpreted the play as "symbolical of the liberty we all think we possess and find we have none, and all our lives are hedged in by social formalities which we fear to break through." He thought John MacDonagh performed well as Dr Westbrook and there were good cameo parts, notably J Anthony Meagher as Black, Pádraig Ó Seacháin as Higgins and Noel Purcell as Doolan. Noel recalled that he thought Máire Nic Shiubhlaigh was also in the cast. He was also dimly aware of something decidedly strange being plotted as, on more than one occasion, he saw a few very blue .45 revolvers being passed around back stage. Only later did it dawn upon him that these were the beginnings of preparations for the Easter Rising. "I had never seen a blue revolver before," said Noel. "I thought they were all chromium plated like the ones the cowboys had in the pictures up in the De Luxe."

Back in the Gaiety on Easter Monday, 24 April 1916, Noel was on school holidays and was helping the D'Oyly Carte advance carpenter to set the stage for that evening's performance of *The Gondoliers* when someone dashed in and said there was bloody murder going on outside in St Stephen's Green. "We all dashed out," said Noel, "to see what was happening and there were these fellows, some of them in uniform—green jackets and hats with the brims turned up at the side, like you'd see the Australian fellas wear; some fellows had only bandoliers around them and others had Sam Browne belts. They didn't look like an army at all. They were making through the big gate at the top of Grafton Street into the Green. Martin Murphy, Leicester Tunks, Henry Lytton, Fred Billington and myself were standing at Noblett's corner looking at all this, having a good gawk. Suddenly from out of nowhere, a hand came out through the bushes behind the iron railing round the green holding a gun, a shiny one, and it went off with a bang. I looked up and there was a policeman lying on the footpath. Of course it frightened the life out of us but we went over to him outside of a place called "Buttercream" and the policeman was bleeding from the mouth. When you're bleeding from the mouth you're either dying or dead and that policeman's number was in the frame. Anyway there was a few more shots fired and, of course, we ran like blazes down King Street."

Noel continued his story of that Easter Week when the theatre was forced to stay closed and the D'Oyly Carte season cancelled. "Martin Murphy was an extraordinary man. He knew everybody and he used to entertain his important friends in the carpenter's shop off the stage. He'd have the most delightful clients in there. That was the place for the intelligentsia. You'd walk into the Master of the Rolls or the Count Markievicz and his little pal, Dubronski, a Polish Jew, drinking bottles of Guinness that cost two and a half pennies—I know because I used to have to go and get it for them. There would be the managers from some of the shops and businesses around the area and there was Joe Cahill who was a fella, that winter or summer, he never took off his overcoat. But he was the fella that invented the two-speed gear for bicycles—Raleigh and Premier bikes. These were all clients that used to be in the carpenter's shop. Oh yes, and the fella that carved the tombstones under the railway arch down in Pearse Street. Martin lived in William Street and on the Tuesday or Wednesday of that week, he sends for me and tells me to get all the seven-by-one timber out of the carpenter's shop and bring it down Tangier Lane into Grafton Street. 'We're going to board up the windows to prevent looting,' Martin tells me. I thought that we were going to board up Louis Wine's jewellery shop or Wests where there was stuff worth thousands of pounds on display or Kapp and Petersons where there were beautiful cherrywood pipes and meerschaums. And where did we board up? Woolworths! Woolworths! They had nothing in their windows priced over sixpence. Why did Martin do it? Well, the answer is very simple—he was a personal friend of the manager!"

Noel had been left fatherless when Pierce Purcell died in 1912. (Pierce had another son, Thomas, by a previous marriage who fought in France in the First World War and this step-brother later lived and died in America.) Consequently, Martin Murphy seems to have assumed some responsibility for the boy and he and Harry Morrison advised Noel that there was no real future for him as a stage-hand and they arranged for Arthur Bex to take him on as an apprentice joiner. AH Bex were shop-fitters in South King Street near the Gaiety and Noel served a seven-year apprenticeship, but he was earning the full rate of pay after only five years because he was so good at the job.

Noel recalled: "I was really a better bench-hand than I was a joiner and carpenter. In the twenties I made all Clerys' glass display cabinets with brass rails. I did them all on my own and it took me nearly a year to do it. I used to go in and have a look at them until fairly recently and they are still perfect—not one mitre gave way." Years later when he became famous, he called into Bex one morning to say "Hello" to the new generation of shop-fitters. Recalling his own time there he said: "The Dublin we had then was very poor. There weren't many spare quids knocking around. It was tough and you had to work hard for very little money, but a great place to be in if you had a little cash. The war was on then and a lot of our fellows, the cream of our young men, were at Mons; what was left of them was sent to the Dardanelles, and be janey, very few of them came back. We called them the "dirty shirts" here but all over the world they were respected as the Dublin Fusiliers. They even wrote a song about them."

During the course of his apprenticeship, Noel took a keen participating interest in what appears to have been a craze at the time, playing hockey on roller skates in the Plaza Ballroom in Abbey Street, which was noted for the spectacular waterfall in its foyer and was situated where the Adelphi Cinema now stands. He was also a regular variety turn at St Theresa's Temperance Hall in Clarendon Street, which achieved world fame when the theatrical history books came to be written as the cradle of the Abbey Theatre. It was the work of the inspired brothers WG and Frank Fay, who began producing Irish plays there around 1902, that gave the theatre its distinction. Their productions were seen and approved by WB Yeats and Lady Gregory and when finance was guaranteed by Miss Horniman of Manchester, the eventual outcome was the construction of the Abbey Theatre, the architect of which was the aforementioned Joseph Holloway. The Fays as producers and meticulous elocutionists alone would have been an asset to the new Abbey Players, but they also brought with them from the St Theresa's Hall such great early actors and actresses as Dudley Digges, Máire Nic Shiubhlaigh (Marie Walker), PJ Kelly and the superb Sara Allgood.

Noel was, by this time, building quite a reputation for himself in the amateur field and the following piece by MAT from the old *Evening Mail*, some time in the late forties, is of interest:

Once upon a time

A card nearly thirty years old has come into my possession. Printed on it are these words: "St Theresa's Total Abstinence Association, Clarendon Street. The Dramatic Society Produce their annual pantomime, *Jack the Giant Killer*. Written and produced by M Guzman, late of the Royal Illusion Company, on St Stephen's Night 1921. Stage Manager, Mr Noel Purcell. Business Manager, Mr L Conroy."

You didn't know that our dear mutual friend Noel was so much of an old stager, huh? Well, it just shows you that his superb mastery of stagecraft is not a mushroom growth sort of thing. This particular panto was taken lots of places, including Gormanstown Camp and the cast had a military escort back in the small hours of the morning (troubled times, you remember).

I daresay the name of M Guzman will awaken many memories too. He was a master of mystic arts; he still is, for that matter.

In the 1922–3 season, Noel was at a different venue. The *Evening Herald* carried a display advertisement for the Everyman Theatre (Rotunda Buildings, Cavendish Row) announcing the second edition of *Jack the Giant Killer* starring Noel Purcell as Weary Willie. No other names are mentioned. It is of interest to note that the Everyman Theatre, later renamed the National Theatre, is the present-day world-famous Gate Theatre, but the stage was situated at the opposite end of the hall to where it is now.

He appeared also in the Father Mathew Hall and in pantomime at the CYMS Harrington Street in which he appeared as characters called "Little Johnny Stout", a deliberate comic misnomer as Noel was by now six foot four and as thin as a lath.

He would return occasionally to the Gaiety in the evenings if there was a big show on and work as a prop man or scene-shifter—"for the extra few bob and the crack." Although he did not drink at that time, he would go over to Neary's through Tangier Lane at the back of the theatre with the other stage hands where the Master of the Rolls or at the other extreme, the Bird Flanagan, might be seen. According to Noel, the Bird Flanagan was a hundred per cent genuine Dublin character. He was the world's worst British soldier because they couldn't get a uniform to fit him. He always looked comical and did outrageously comical things too. Incidentally, Flanagan is reputed to have earned his nick-name "The Bird" as a result of a prank he played on a DMP Sergeant called Ryan. Flanagan went into a poulterers in Moore Street and bought a turkey which he had labelled with his name and gave instructions that the bird was to be hung on a hook on a display-bar outside the shop and he would pick it up later. He concealed himself in a doorway until he spied his old adversary, Sergeant Ryan, passing on his beat. Flanagan dashed out in full view of the policeman and snatched the turkey hanging outside the shop. A hot-footed pursuit ensued until Flanagan had his collar felt in O'Connell Street. Quite a crowd joined the procession back to the poulterers in Moore Street where, of course, Flanagan had irrefutable proof that the bird was, in fact, his property. A contemporary of the Bird Flanagan was the "Toucher" Doyle, but it is superfluous to explain the origin of his nickname.

"I remember the time," recalled Noel, "when the Bird Flanagan, bless his soul, brought a corpse into Neary's over his shoulders. Out of the cab and into the bar he came, pushed him against the partition and said, 'I just thought yez would like to have a drink with him before he's planted.' Drinks were drunk, the repartee was as fine as a barman's wit and the Bird, having omitted to pay for any of the drinks, picked up your man, put him back in the cab and held his hand all the way back to the City Morgue."

In 1926 the city of Philadelphia was celebrating the 150th year since the signing of the Declaration of Independence in 1776 and a Great Exhibition was planned, the centre-piece of which would be the now famous long-count fight between Jack Dempsey and Gene Tunney at the Sesquicentennial Stadium on 23 September. Over in Dublin, a certain cabinet-making part-time stage performer called Noel Purcell was anxious to see the affair. So he packed his kit of tools and announced that he was "off to Philadelphia in the morning." When he arrived there he looked for a job as a joiner and got it. He worked at a bench between a German and a Pole, and conversation was such that the silence was deafening, but it was worth it for the enjoyment of the fight. After looking at as much of America as could be seen from a work bench, he concluded that he didn't like it half as much as he had liked the fight and, as it would be panto time again soon in Dublin, he packed his bags and arrived home in time for rehearsals at the CYMS.

Here he was supported by Pete Davis (on another occasion he referred to a Pete McDonagh) whom he described as a very funny comedian who died, unfortunately, of a bad chest, or a bad "east and west" as Noel described it. The show was seen by Tom Powell who had been the apothecary in Clerys and became the manager of Brown Thomas, the department store. Powell took over the Olympia once every year to present a variety show. In 1928 he and his partner, Harry Byrne, found that they were short of a tall performer to appear in a boxing sketch. They remembered Noel and offered him the booking at two pounds ten shillings for the week. So Noel did his normal job during the day and appeared at the Olympia twice a night. In the sketch, the principal comedian, Chris Sylvester, thought he was going to fight a half dying little man but the referee used to announce that "owing to indisposition the Basher wouldn't be able to appear, but at enormous expense they had secured the services of Sledgehammer Bill." Noel remembered with a laugh, "In spite of everything, I used to get the tar beat out of me with the long gloves—comedy gloves y'know."

This appearance led to Noel's working for Tom Powell later in the year in the 1928–9 pantomime season at the Queen's as Will Atkins, the pirate king, in *Robinson Crusoe* which was produced by Wally Black with a mainly cross-channel cast. According to Noel it wasn't a particularly funny show but he got his share of laughs which were attributed by Lorcan Bourke, the part proprietor of the theatre, to the fact that Noel's appearance would make a cat laugh. His long extremely skinny legs were encased in black tights and these were topped by a short pirate's skirt and hat. He also peppered his script with Dublinese like "Don't act the maggot!" The English members of the cast didn't have a clue what he was talking about but the Irish punters loved it.

All over Dublin, Noel's beautiful joinery work could be appreciated in the most fashionable shops and department stores. Now, as a result of his appearance in the Queen's pantomime, Jimmy O'Dea and Harry O'Donovan had their eyes on him and soon Dubliners would be seeing work from him of a different aspect, on the professional stage. Still Noel was always very proud of his display cases and glass counters. Years later, when he was sharing top-of-the-bill with Jimmy O'Dea at the Theatre Royal, they were having a drink one morning in the very distinctive Scotch House, now demolished. "You know, Jimmy," said Noel, "this place was originally designed by a fellow, Fred Jeffs [There was an actor of this name who once appeared in silent films with O'Dea] just after the First World War. We had terrible problems, we were here so long that Mr Foley, the owner, used to say— 'Heh, heh! That fellow grew up here!' talking about me and I'm six foot four. 'Yes,' says Mr Foley, 'He was only a youngster when he came to work here.'"

CHAPTER TWO

The O'Dea-O'Donovan company (O'D Productions) which was formed in 1927 was presenting its second pantomime *Little Red Riding Hood* at the Queen's Theatre in the Christmas season of 1929 and they offered Noel the role of Dame Longshanks (who else?), grandmother to Red Riding Hood. This was to be Noel's first dame role; previously in amateur productions he used to fall around the stage in comedy routines but he had never been in skirts before. Red Riding Hood was played by twelve-year-old Eileen Marmion, a seasoned little trouper who had graduated from the Aileen Lennox Magee stage school some years earlier. She had played the part of a Teddy Bear in O'D Productions' first panto *Sinbad the Sailor* at the Olympia a year earlier, but the part of Red Riding Hood was better fitted to her talents. Eileen was born in January 1918 at 3 North King Street where her family had a fruit and vegetable business. She normally went to school at King's Inns Street. Her mother, Mary (Mamie), née Ennis, who died in November 1979 aged eighty-seven, was a Dublin woman who had been employed at Eason's book shop for a time until she was obliged to chaperone her young daughter on her theatrical engagements. Eileen's father, Patrick Marmion, was born in 1892 and died aged twenty-seven in 1919 when she was only eighteen months old. He had been a school teacher.

Eileen had started her stage career in shows which Harry O'Donovan had produced prior to his collaboration with Jimmy O'Dea in the Olympia in Dublin, the Palace in Cork and tours around Ireland. Noel said of her, "She was a lovely child and I thought she was an exceptionally talented little thing. And that's all I thought—at the time." They met for the first time at a script conference in Harry's house in Baggot Street and Eileen thought that Noel was gorgeous but he was so tall and so thin that he reminded her of an animated telegraph pole. And Noel agreed: "I was so thin that I used to drink olive oil in an attempt to put on weight." The critics acclaimed their partnership and the *Evening Herald* noted in January 1930:

> As Little Red Riding Hood, Eileen Marmion had an important part, and the manner in which she portrayed it would have reflected credit on a much older and more experienced actress. Noel Purcell as Dame Longshanks added much to the fun of the performance and was quite a success in a rather difficult role.

Noel was offered a salary of £8 a week. "Good money in those days," Noel said. "Come to think of it, very good money in view of the fact that before that I was getting £4 2s 7d for a forty-seven-hour week and that was as a gaffer in the cabinetmaking. So when I was asked, I stayed with the O'D Company playing straight man to Jimmy. We got on very well together and looked really funny on the stage. We complemented each other, what with me being six foot four and him only five foot four, we looked like Goliath and...Lester Piggot."

In his eagerness, like O'Dea and O'Donovan, fully to embrace the all-consuming love and passion of his life, it is doubtful if Noel gave much thought to the future of his chosen profession in a type of entertainment that was already dying. Indeed it is doubtful if it occurred to any of them in the endless hurly-burly of writing and memorising and staging fresh material that they were making a unique artistic contribution to society. Very few serious writers with the exception of Bernard Shaw, Max Beerbohm and a few others, ever bothered to analyse the significance of the institution of the music-hall, which in the form it had originally evolved was virtually dead by 1920. But it did not die ignominiously. James Joyce paid a visit to London with his father John in May 1900 and they spent most of their evenings at the music-halls. On his return home, James announced oracularly to his brother Stanislaus, "The music-hall, not poetry, is a criticism of life." Puncturing old solemnities and making new ones was a favourite diversion with him and he was pleased then as always to find value in what he was expected to condemn as commonplace and vulgar.

By Noel's and Jimmy O'Dea's time, music-hall had been replaced by revue and what came to be known as variety or cine-variety (a mixture of stage show and film), which included acts like jugglers, acrobats, wire-walkers, trick cyclists and such like, whose origins were more firmly rooted in the circus. Dance bands whose popularity originated on radio very often appeared at the top of the bill. Comedians with magnetic and sympathetic personalities could preserve the genuine core of music-hall for a time but they had to be good.

Imagine Noel Purcell, thin and unbelievably, ridiculously tall for the dame role he impersonates in the most delightfully flat, but strangely musical, almost velvet-like Dublin accent. (Noel when playing low comedy made no attempt to disguise his accent; in fact he exaggerated it.) His height is accentuated when Red Riding Hood comes on the scene and if one allows the mind to wander it is only to engage in an imaginary estimate of how many yards of material it must have taken to clothe Granny Purcell! The fact that such minutiae engage one's interest in him is an indication of the awakening recognition that this new potentially great personality should with a few expertly directed strokes of the spokeshave become a great entertainer.

Noel had a solo spot in the panto which he performed in front of a space-restricting front cloth in his dame costume and on roller skates. Because of the steep rake in the Queen's stage, this gave rise to alarm to the musical director and his musicians who each night fully expected Noel to come flying over the footlights on top of them in the orchestra pit.

The season ended in February and the panto moved on to Cork where they were so successful that the O'D company decided to remain at the Palace in a new revue that they had been rehearsing called *Irish Smiles*. Noel set his dame's wig aside for this revue and the eagle-eyed O'Dea noticed that Noel's hair was greying slightly at the temples which he found unacceptable for anyone playing comedy and advised Noel to use henna on the offending locks in order to darken them. The smallest detail of every show was of absorbing interest to O'Dea—the dialogue had to be whistle clean and he would not tolerate a speck of dirt on a costume. "He was a very fussy little man," said Noel, "and he wasn't nicknamed 'Napoleon' for nothing." (See *Jimmy O'Dea, the Pride of the Coombe* for details)

The new revue was a success and according to one reviewer:

> Noel Purcell with a baritone of good range, sang "Somebody Pushed Me" a humorous ballad. It was well received and created a good deal of humour.

Eileen Marmion had performed song-and-dance routines with Harry O'Donovan (known affectionately as HOD) in the past. With her new partner Noel Purcell she had a particularly successful routine in which, dressed in a tutu, she emerged from a large chocolate box, centre stage, and sang and danced with Noel in a number called "Betty the Breaker of Hearts" which ended with Noel carrying her off-stage perched on his shoulder. Eileen, despite her tender years, devised all her own vocal and dancing arrangements. She and Noel figured in many little cameos, written especially for them by HOD, such as the following which has somehow survived.

"Would You Like to Take a Walk" (1930)

[*NOEL is sitting on park seat, reading magazine. He looks at his watch. Enter EILEEN with dolls pram. She strolls past him.*]

EILEEN [*As she passes*]: Good Morning.

N: Good Morning.

E [*Turning back*]: Waiting for something to turn up?

N: Yes...No!

E: Too bad your girl is late.

N: Go on. Pass on.

E: Women are awful aren't they? [*He reads magazine*] Our nurse loves you.

N: Indeed? How nice.

E: She says skinny men fascinate her.

N: I told you to get along. [*Reads magazine*].

E: What are you reading?

N: Longfellow's poems.

E: Did you write them?

N: I said Longfellow.

E: He couldn't have been longer than you surely.

N: Go away. [*Reads*]

E: My father has a motor car.

N: By Jove!

E: No, by instalments. [*Grins*] You bought that one, didn't you? What do you do for a living?

N: I work.

E: That's unusual, isn't it?

N: Is it?

E: My father does no work.

N [*Reading*]:...Hm.

E: That's so that mother won't be sick.

N: So that mother won't be sick?

E: Yes. She told Auntie that she'd throw a fit if he got a job.

N: [*Looks at watch on and off*]

E: My father loves water on Sundays.

N: Oh. He swims on Sundays?

E: No. He gets up terribly early and drinks all the water out of the wash-jug.

N: Oh. I see.

E: I put four pinkeens in the jug last Saturday.

N: Great Scott!

E: He only drank two of them.

N: Run home. You make me ill.

E: Looks like your girl is giving you the frozen mitt.

N: Where do you pick up those expressions?

E: My sister. She's a terrible necker.

N: Necker!

E: She works.

N: Glad some of the family is industrious.

E: She's a gold digger. Her young man digs too.

N: What does he dig?

E: I don't know but Daddy won't let her marry him because he digs with the wrong foot.

N: [*Laughs behind magazine*]

E: Well. Good morning.

N: No. Don't go. I'm beginning to like you.

E: Wait 'til I park the pram.

[*She puts pram beside seat as music begins. Song and Dance*]

In another little cameo called "Truth Comes..." Eileen tells her big sister's young man (Noel) a few shattering home truths about the light of his life. Eileen has the final line in this sketch when she asks Noel: "Why don't you wait until I grow up and marry me!" Did Harry O'Donovan have a prophetic instinct about something which hadn't, of course, even occurred to Noel or Eileen?

Golden-haired Eileen was a completely ingenuous child performer. Shortly after at a time when there were hundreds of carbon-copy Shirley Temples, she did not have the sickly precociousness that characterised them. There was no touch of that automatic, mindlessly over-rehearsed movement so noticeable in most child performers—whichever way she moved on the stage she knew exactly why she did it. The quick smile, the quizzical look, the lifting of an eyebrow—all these were spontaneous, a natural technical perfection allied to an attractive personality, that strange elusive quality that pervades an entire theatre. Sweet, pretty and petite were adjectives that had been bestowed upon her by the press, but they were merely icing on the cake and the young actress, Miss Marmion, could have done equally well without them.

The O'D company hadn't been aware that one of their performances of *Little Red Riding Hood* had been seen at the Queen's by DJ Clarke, the shrewd and respected manager of the Argyle Theatre, Birkenhead, who on his return to England strongly recommended the O'D company to Sir Oswald Stoll, one of the most powerful men in the variety theatre in Britain, and chairman of the Number One Stoll circuit. A representative of the Stoll organisation crossed over to Cork and saw a performance of *Irish Smiles*, the result of which was a week's engagement as a try-out at the Ardwick Empire (later renamed the Manchester Hippodrome) which, if successful, would lead to an engagement at the prestigious Shepherd's Bush Empire, London. Eileen wasn't aware of any special business arrangements but Noel told her many years later that the offer was subject to her appearance in the shows.

Irish Smiles played the Ardwick Empire in May 1930 and such was its success that it was booked for the entire Stoll circuit. The show began when the front tabs were held open for Eileen and she came on in front of the footlights with her back to the tabs, and in those days without microphones, she sang over a fifteen piece orchestra the opening song:

> If I had a great treasure, if I had a great prize,
> Gladly I'd trade them for your smiling Irish eyes.
> There are stars in the heavens but who'd ever surmise,
> That they were created for your smiling Irish eyes.
> Although the greatest distance may lie between us two,
> Sweetheart, my whole existence depends completely on you.
> There's a wonderful colour like the blue of the skies,
> Angels have made it for your smiling Irish eyes.

The front tabs were raised revealing the Odee dancing troupe who performed an Irish dance and the show was under way.

After the Shepherd's Bush engagement Sir Oswald Stoll decided to feature a sketch from the show in his premier theatre, London's showpiece, the Coliseum, which in those days ranked above the Palladium. The Coliseum, now the permanent home of the English National Opera Company, is one of the most beautiful theatres in Britain. Designed by Frank Matcham, the theatre architect responsible for many now demolished Empires, Hippodromes and Palaces, it had many unusual innovations: a mobile lounge to take royal parties to their boxes, post-office facilities in the foyer, and the first revolving stage in Britain with three revolves that moved independently. Harry O'Donovan related that on one occasion when he was making an announcement he stood inadvertently on the edge of one of the revolves only to find himself being whisked unceremoniously into the wings. In the late forties the Coliseum's revolving stage was dismantled, never to be used again.

Top of the bill in September 1930 were: Jose Collins, Phyllis Neilson-Terry and Company in *The Interlude of War*, Jimmy O'Dea and Harry O'Donovan and Company, and Billy Bennett. Noel had last met Jose Collins and Phyllis Neilson-Terry years previously when he was a call-boy at the Gaiety. The O'D company presented a sketch called "Micky Breaks into America", described by *The*

Stage as "starring Jimmy O'Dea and a company with a difference."
The cast was:

Doctor...Harry O'Donovan
Italian...Tom Dunne
Gentleman...Chas O'Reilly
Dublin Man...Noel Purcell
Girl...Connie Ryan
Micky...Jimmy O'Dea

The action took place at Ellis Island with Jimmy using every stratagem at his disposal, mainly the gift of the gab, to gain admission to the USA. The comedy received a tumultuous reception and Stoll re-booked the company for a second appearance at the Coliseum in November. It was a remarkable achievement for the O'D company, most of whom had only lately turned fully professional, and yet they had secured two bookings within three months at one of the outstanding variety theatres in the world—an unattainable dream for thousands of performers who had spent a lifetime on the halls.

In the meantime the company appeared at Sheffield, Birkenhead, Aston, Aldershot and all the important local London halls. Noel and Eileen were pulling their weight as is evidenced by a review in a Bristol newspaper:

Bristol Hippodrome this week is as Irish as an enterprising management and a clever company can make it. *Irish Smiles* is a bright little show, clean, competent and often clever...Jimmy O'Dea is a natty little comedian, but the honours go to Eileen Marmion, a tiny flaxen-haired girl with a surprising voice and an amazing stage presence. She plays in a sketch "Truth Comes..." with Noel Purcell which is the smartest thing in the show...

Although Eileen was being chaperoned by her mother, Noel took it upon himself to accompany the youngster to school each morning. Schooling for children in touring companies was required by law. As a London County Council bye-law put it:

> In consequence of the special educational disadvantages to which children in theatrical touring companies are exposed, the Board of Education have made a statutory requirement that a person in charge of every child so employed shall keep a record of the scheme of work on which he (she) is engaged at school and that these records shall be produced, if required, to the Authority of any area in which the licence takes effect or to the teacher of a school which the child attends...

Eileen attended dozens of schools and the official observations as to her progress were excellent:

> "Progress very satisfactory."
> "Very intelligent and easily adapts herself to her work."
> "Adaptable and intelligent."
> "Intelligent and keenly interested in her work."
> "Very much above average."

Noel adopted Eileen as a sort of mascot, taking her to school and escorting her home from the theatre. If he happened to be ready to leave first in the evenings he would shout into the girls' dressing room, "Are you ready, Jemmy?" The origin of the nickname "Jemmy" is a mystery even to Eileen. Sometimes he called her "Whiskers." He used these to differentiate between her and two or three other Eileens in the Odee girls, one of whom was Eileen Phelan who worked later in the Queen's and married Kevin Bourke of the famous Dublin theatrical family.

He even took Eileen to the cinema—with his girl friends! "I didn't mind at all," she says, "but I was a bit puzzled by the looks and the remarks I would get from his girl friends."

When the company were arranging to play the second Coliseum date in November they discovered that the excerpts from *Irish Smiles* would be in three sections and that Eileen's and Noel's routine was to be included. No 4 on the programme read:

Jimmy O'Dea and Harry O'Donovan present:
"Micky Tries Matrimony" Written by Harry O'Donovan
[*Scene 1—Micky Proposes*]
The American...Harry O'Donovan
His Wife...Vera Elson
Ned Turley...Chas O'Reilly
Marie...Connie Ryan
Micky...Jimmy O'Dea

Little Eileen Marmion with Noel Purcell will appear between Scenes One and Two in an excerpt from the O'Dea-O'Donovan Revue *Irish Smiles*.

Scene Two—The Legal Separation
(Marie and Micky find Married Life Trying)

Billy Bennett, who billed himself as "Almost a Gentleman," was once again in the show with them. Dressed in an ill-fitting suit of tails, a dickey which left his midriff exposed and huge army boots, sporting a walrus moustache and hair parted in the middle and plastered down at each side, he delivered surrealist type monologues of his own composition, such as the one about "The Miser":

A bird once flew in at his window;
It had flown all the way from Iraq.
He plucked it of all its feathers
And made it walk all the way back.

Billy lived opposite the stage door of the Coliseum and when it came close to his entrance during the three performances daily, the stage-door keeper would telephone across to him and tell him, "You're on, Billy!"

There is a show business story which has been attributed to many different comedians. Noel Purcell swore that, in fact, the originator was Billy Bennett. Noel, Eileen and Billy were standing in the wings one evening watching another act on the bill known as The Hai-Yung Family who were described in their billing matter as "Acrobats, Jugglers, Contortionists, Top Spinners, Balancers and Hair Raisers." At one point in the act, one member was hanging by his teeth on to the pigtail of a second member—all very spectacular stuff, but Billy Bennett was unimpressed; he turned to Noel and muttered gruffly, but with a twinkle in his eye, "All that fuckin' messing about just because they're too bloody lazy to learn a comic song!"

JB Priestley observed in *Lost Empires*, "As soon as the English go to music halls they love the Irish." Colin MacInnes expanded more deeply on the theme in *Sweet Saturday Night*:

The cases of Whittle and of George Formby Senior may remind us that, as the century advanced, provincial artists were being made more welcome at the heartland of the halls, in London. There was evidently a lot of audience resistance to overcome here, for it seems there have always been, in the popular theatre, curious fashions as to which regions are either "funny" or, at any rate, full of "character", and which are not; and it required considerable perseverance by successful artists to establish any such region in the popular fancy. Ten years ago for instance [1957], Liverpool speech and people weren't considered specially interesting let alone admirable, when lo and behold there came the Beatles, Ken Dodd, and the whole Merseyside vogue, so that Liverpudlians suddenly became persons of fascination, even glamour. Thirty years before, in the late 1920s, Gracie Fields had made Lancashire seem a place infinitely desirable and all its "lasses" as admirable as she.*

Thus it was that artists from outside London had not only to project themselves, but wherever it was they came from. As one might expect, the earliest non-London characters to be accepted as automatically of theatrical interest were the Irish. Part of the myth that arose from the English oppression of Ireland was that "Paddy" was a quaint, illogical, endearing fellow, full of "blarney" and inconsequence. Thus, from the early beginning of music hall, Sam Collins was singing "Paddy's Wedding" and "Limerick Races." Before his death in 1865, WG Ross (although born in Glasgow) had "Pat's Leather Breeches" among his earlier songs. So strong did this tradition of theatrical Irishness become that as we have seen, Harry Lauder—that epitome of the Scot!—had initially to present himself to English audiences as an Irishman. The Celtic stream soon became a flood, with such later numbers as Lily Lassah's "Molly, My Irish Molly" and Ella Retford "Irish, and Proud of It Too"—the tone now being less comical and more sentimental and aggressive. The whole thing got quite out of hand in "Dancing 'Neath the Irish Moon" sung by Dainty Daisy Dormer (1883-1947). There was even later the absurdity of an artist like Talbot O'Farrell singing "Mother Machree" and "When Irish Eyes Are Smiling" to enrapture English audiences, despite his name not being O'Farrell and his English birthplace far from the Emerald Isle. All Londoners could do in retaliation was to mock this spate of Irishry, as in Dan Leno's satirical "Mrs Kelly".*

---

* Gracie was playing the Palladium when the O'D company were at the Coliseum and Noel and Eileen dashed across London one evening to catch her act.

* Leno himself had spent some time in Dublin and acquired a Dublin accent so that he was mistaken for a genuine Irishman, and for a while billed himself as such. A gramophone recording of his "Mrs Kelly" monologue survives from 1901 and is surprisingly undated.

Mr MacInnes also notes that none of the themes of contemporary Irish songs dealing with the famine, the tenant wars or the Easter Rising, filtered, even in diluted form, into the English halls.

There could be no doubting the popularity of the O'D company which toured England and Scotland regularly before the war, returning home each year to present a revue and a pantomime at the Olympia. Noel's salary had risen to £10 a week and he sent money home regularly to his mother who had by now retired from the antique business. Some of the sketches in which Noel appeared with Jimmy became classics and were often repeated. "Mine's a Pint", "Seeing Him Off", "The Last Drink" and "Fresh Fish" were particular favourites.

Noel was the bandit, Fatty, in *Babes in the Wood* at the Olympia in 1930–1. He was dame again in *Dick Whittington* in 1931–2. He was Buttons in the 1932–3 production of *Cinderella* with Ouida McDermott, a familiar face from his call-boy days in the Gaiety, as Prince Charming. Jimmy O'Dea played dame again in the next two seasons in *Mother Goose* and *Red Riding Hood*, giving Noel male roles, but Noel was back as dame in *Jack and the Beanstalk* in the 1935–6 season. In the last O'D pantomime at the Olympia in 1936–7, *Ali Baba and the Forty Thieves*, Noel played Abdulla, the captain of the thieves.

The relationship between Noel, Jimmy and especially HOD was excellent. But it was a fact that Jimmy had a slightly sadistic streak both verbally and physically. He developed the habit of slapping and punching people on the stage in what he, no doubt, regarded as his own variation of the ancient "slapstick." Noel decided he wasn't going to tolerate any of this behaviour and one night just as Jimmy was about to strike, Noel timed his retaliatory movement by pointing his raised and crooked elbow at Jimmy who ended up with an extremely painful Adam's apple. In 1933 Noel was received into the Order of the Knights of Columbanus; membership was quite an honour and direct attempts at membership were forbidden. His proposer was Jimmy O'Dea and his seconder was Harry O'Donovan.

The favoured relaxation after a year of touring and resident seasons was a summer cruise. The White Star Line's cruising steamer *Homeric* which sailed from Southampton to the Mediterranean, Italy, Sicily, Dalmatian Coast, North Africa and Malta was favoured on several occasions. In 1933 the party included Rev Michael Allen, Mr and Mrs James A O'Dea, Mr and Mrs Harry O'Donovan, Mr and Mrs Edward Twomey, Miss Kathleen Simpson and Mr Noel Purcell. On the eighth of June 1933 it chanced to be Fr Allen's birthday so the chief steward had a special menu printed in his honour wishing him many happy returns of the day. The menu was the source of some amusement:

Grapefruit O'Dea

Potage Twomey

Sole O'Donovan

Chicken à la Simpson

Pommes Purcell

Birthday Cake

Bombe Allen

Nookey à la Ernest Shannon

Café à la Toboggan

Cruising Steamer *Homeric*   8 June 1933.

Mícheál Mac Liammóir once described a dinner given in honour of the Gate Theatre company after a performance of *Hamlet* in Elsinore, Denmark, and when he perused the menu he found to his chagrin that the sweet course had been named "Raspberries Mac Liammóir"; one wonders what Jimmy O'Dea's thoughts were upon his association with a grapefruit.

In 1934 they began filming their first movie *Jimmy Boy* for Baxter and Barter at Cricklewood in which Noel had a good featured role. In 1937 O'D productions arranged with the great impresario, Louis Elliman, to do two shows a year at the Gaiety Theatre, Dublin. There would be a revue in August to coincide with Horse Show Week and a pantomime at Christmas. Noel appeared as usual in the sketches in the first show *Gaiety Revels of 1937* and he looked resplendent in a white period costume and tricorne hat as the admiral in *Mother Goose* that Christmas. In the same year O'D productions set up their own film unit to make their second film *Blarney* in which Noel appeared as a Garda sergeant. He was, with Tom Dunne, one of the ugly sisters in the 1938–9 season's panto *Cinderella*.

There now occurred a turning point in Noel's career (as there did for many following the declaration of war in 1939); during the run of *Cinderella* Noel asked for an increase in salary of £5 per week. It wasn't an unreasonable sum in view of the fact that when cross-channel performers were engaged to appear, their salaries were far in excess of those received by local artists. Furthermore the O'D shows were breaking records at the Gaiety. There was much debate about this salary increase and eventually a mutually acceptable compromise was agreed upon. Instead of paying Noel an extra £5 for the run of the panto, he would be paid £2 10s and this increase would extend to the rest of the year. At the end of the Dublin run the panto was taken on a tour of the major Irish dates, but when Noel checked his salary after the first week in Limerick he found that the promised increase was not included. He discussed this with the company manager, JC Browner, who replied, "That's all there is." Noel was as straight as a die and his word was his bond. It is possible that the company business manager had forgotten the agreement, but whoever was responsible, Noel couldn't understand a deficiency in straight dealing in others. He informed Browner that if he didn't receive the money in Cork he wouldn't go on to Liverpool, and when the cash didn't materialise he just departed without a word to anyone.

Noel decided to go to New York to see the World's Fair and

was joined by his great friend Maxie Elliman, manager of the Theatre Royal. "We were like brothers," Noel recalled. The Elliman family, headed by the father Maurice as chairman, took over the Royal in 1936. Louis was managing director and producer, Abe was general manager and booked the films and Maxie, after a spell at running the Corinthian, was house manager. In New York they attended all the big Broadway shows and saw Cab Calloway and many of the other big names of the time. Back in Dublin, the alarm bells were ringing; O'D productions were anxious to feature Noel in their August 1939 show but when they quizzed Eileen Marmion as to his whereabouts, they discovered that he was in America and not particularly interested in O'D productions.

When Noel returned later in the year, he took up a week's engagement at the Theatre Royal playing straight man to the eccentric comic and later acknowledged interpreter of the works of Samuel Beckett, "Professor Walloffski" himself, Max Wall. During the Christmas season 1939–40, Noel, as dame, starred with Frank O'Donovan and Dick Forbes in *Robinson Crusoe* at the Queen's. During the run of the show, another member of the cast, Bert Lena, described to Noel the symptoms of his daughter's sudden illness and Noel recognised them as being similar to those suffered by his own younger sister before she died of diphtheria, and urged Lena to get his child to a doctor immediately. She escaped the tragic fate of Noel's sister, and Lena was inexpressibly grateful to him.

When the O'D company went into rehearsals for their Horse Show Week revue *Gaiety Revels of 1940* Noel consented to appear in the show at the request of Maurice Elliman who was an old friend of his mother. That was Noel's final appearance with the O'D company at the Gaiety but he did work with Jimmy O'Dea again in some of their well-known sketches when they shared top-billing some years later at the Theatre Royal where Noel had established himself as resident comedian.

Noel Purcell was a man completely without guile, who never

was heard to utter an unkind word about anyone. He was one of nature's gentlemen and he held no animosity towards the O'D company. In fact he regarded the whole business "over a couple of pounds" as extremely lucky for him. Had he received the money he might never have left the O'D company and might have missed the opportunity to extend his range in that open-hearted down-to-earth humour which made him one of the unmistakable voices of Dublin in his own right.

CHAPTER THREE

In the early 1940s Noel worked more or less as a freelance performer. Dónal Giltenan (who years later wrote a show about Percy French called *The Golden Years* in which Milo O'Shea was delightful as Phil the Fluter) wrote some material for him which he used on tours. In May of 1940, for instance, he presented a show called *Anything May Happen* at the Empire Theatre, Belfast, and the cast included Mary Poswolski, the principal dancer with O'D productions. Noel paid many visits to Belfast and on one occasion he met a young singer called Joe McLaughlin who had the loveliest voice he had ever heard and who asked Noel if he could get him into the Royal at £20 a week. Noel knew that Maxie Elliman wouldn't pay that kind of money—it was just about what Noel was getting himself. Maxie said McLaughlin wasn't worth £20 and offered him £15 which was refused. McLoughlin was discovered by Jimmy O'Dea in 1941 who put him in his show *So What?* at the Gaiety, where he was so popular that he appeared regularly thereafter at the Royal. In 1955 Noel met Joe, now known as Josef Locke, who told him that Louis Elliman was paying him £1100 for an appearance that week at the Royal. Joe had to go to England first to win real recognition and there he became known as "Mr Blackpool" from the resort where he did regular summer seasons. The crack was ninety, of course, as they recalled the days when Maxie Elliman thought hard of paying him £15 a week.

When he was appearing at the Hippodrome, Belfast, in the early forties, Noel met Albert Sharpe (of Walt Disney's *Darby O'Gill and the Little People* fame) and they discussed the idea of a black and white minstrel show for the Royal. Sharpe had toured Ireland in the minstrel show "The Dixies" and Dave Davis, who had worked with him as Massa Johnson, was also available. They sold the idea to Louis Elliman and so the Royal Minstrels were formed. According to Noel it had never been possible to fill the Royal, it was a huge place and there was no intimacy. Even "Schnozzle" Durante couldn't pack it. But from the Minstrel show on, the Royal changed.

In 1941 Noel appeared with Harry Bailey in a show called *Hullabaloo* at the Royal. Bailey had been born into the circus so he set about teaching Noel all sorts of skills that they could use in the comedy routines. Noel became quite adept at juggling, wire-walking, and trick cycling, and of course, he was already an expert on roller skates. Harry Bailey in his act drove everyone mad by announcing that he would play a solo on his square-shaped fiddle and after playing a few notes would proceed to tell another joke. Sometimes these jokes were not exactly compliment-ary to the Jewish race and Bailey would add at the end of his story—"If the boss is in I'm only joking!" He had great affection for Noel of whom he said: "There was something about Noel—you would have to like the man. He was so innocent, he was like a big kid. Nothing was too much trouble for him—he would try anything."

In the Christmas season 1940–1, Noel appeared as dame in his first Theatre Royal pantomime, *Mother Hubbard Goes to Town*, with a cast of 150 and it was directed by Charlie Wade. Freda Bannon, who was then a juvenile performer, recalls that Noel's height was used as part of the comic business, and they used to put a ladder up beside him so that the youngsters could whisper in his ear. Freda adds, "I remember the horror of having to go up this very tall ladder up to this very tall man just to talk to him."

In his personal life, Noel had met Eileen again after an interval of time and, realising how much they had missed each other, began a serious courtship which resulted in Noel proposing marriage outside Switzers of Grafton Street in 1940. ("Grafton Street's a wonderland, there's magic in the air...") He was accepted. Noel's comment on this was, "Eileen waited for me to grow up!" A neat twist on the last line in Harry O'Donovan's prophetic sketch in which Eileen asked Noel to wait for her to grow up and marry her. Noel had saved four hundred pounds towards the great day, but would it be enough? Noel never had a contract with Louis Elliman in all the years they worked together. "And you never had to ask for a raise either," recalled Noel. "It came automatically when business was good." When he and Eileen fixed the date of their marriage for 7 July 1941 in St Michan's Church, Green Street, Noel went to Louis and said, "Hey, do us a favour, Louis, as I'm getting married. Give me a salary of one hundred pounds a week for the next few weeks"—and it was done!

The happy couple planned a quiet wedding without all the show business trappings and ballyhoo. Harry O'Donovan was Noel's best man (and in the course of time godfather to the Purcell's first born) and the matron of honour was Dorothy Goulding, who later married James Joyce's nephew Frederick. But Noel and Eileen soon discovered that their friends in the theatre had no intention of allowing the occasion to pass without due ceremony. Alban Chambers, the cinema organist at the Savoy, took on the duties of master of ceremonies, and A Gordon Spicer, the Compton organist at the Royal, played the church organ and accompanied May Devitt in appropriate hymns. They were married by Noel's old friend Fr Michael Allen and the reception was in the Grand Central Hotel. After the honeymoon in Cork, they took up residence in Newbridge Drive, Sandymount, where they remained for fifteen years. Eileen's mother came to live with them when the family began to arrive. Noel always had a preference for living in Sandymount which appeared to have been based upon his recollections of buying Merrion Strand cockles wrapped in copies of the *Herald* and *Mail* from the cockle man in his childhood. The cockles from the Irishtown end of Sandymount Strand, he remembered, were not so big or succulent because waste water was allowed drain off into that area.

A month before he was married in 1941, Noel had been given a momentous opportunity to display his versatility. Stanley Illsley and Leo McCabe presented the great early Abbey actor Arthur Sinclair as Captain Boyle in a production of Seán O'Casey's *Juno and the Paycock* at the Gaiety and they offered Noel the part of Joxer Daly. Noel rose to the challenge and the theatre critic of *The Standard*, Gabriel Fallon, said of his performance:

> No wonder he enjoyed playing Joxer—a beautifully broad and mellow interpretation, with a drunken slither of genius all its own.

The "drunken slither" refers to the final scene in the play in which Captain Boyle rambles on drunkenly. Noel positioned himself standing straight, with his back against the wall, but as the Captain mumbles on, Noel very slowly, from the knees up, began to slide down the wall helplessly until just before the final curtain falls, he is sitting slumped on the floor.

In the Christmas season of 1941-2, Noel was back at the Royal as one of the Ugly Sisters in *Cinderella* with Mike Nolan, John Lynsky and, making his first appearance at the Royal, Eddie Byrne as Baron Weasel. It is recorded that the script was by a mysterious figure who preferred to be known as "Namille", but since it is clearly "Elliman" spelt backwards it fooled nobody.

In April of 1942, Noel joined Eire O'Reilly, Jimmy Harvey, Mick Eustace (a comedian apparently much influenced by the silent movies of Mack Sennett), Bill Brady (a much underrated and forgotten dame comedian whose timing was needle sharp) and Liam O'Connor in a revue *That's That* at the Queen's. Noel was Mrs Hubbard in *Red Riding Hood* at the Royal in 1942–3. The cast was a strong one with Eddie Byrne, Mike Nolan, Jack Harrington, Ursula Doyle, Seán Mooney, Peggy Dell, JC Browner and the last appearance of the Royal Violettes under the direction of Violet Hindle. But Louis Elliman, or TR Royle, as he preferred to be known professionally, had big plans for the future of the Royal. The TR Royle shows of the following years are the ones by which the theatre is best remembered. Louis Elliman, with the unfailing touch of an impresario of genius, considered, sifted, selected and finally decided upon a team of performers, backed up by first rate technicians backstage, that has never since been equalled.

His principal comedian would be Noel Purcell, supported by the character comedian Eddie Byrne, and their regular accomplice would be Pauline Forbes. This basic comedy team would be augmented as required by Cecil Sheridan and Mickser Reid, Jack Cruise, Michael Clarke, Harry Bailey, Séamus Forde, Michael Ripper, Doris Finn, Norman Barrs, Joe O'Dea and Bob Hennessy. Resident singers would be Seán Mooney and Frankie Blowers but their numbers too would be augmented from time to time by May Devitt, Patricia Black, Peggy Dell, Renée Flynn and Joseph McLaughlin (Josef Locke). There would be two new dance teams. The first was the Royalettes, under the direction of Alice Dalgarno and her partner Babs de Monte, who was no stranger to the Royal as she had appeared with Francis Mangan's troupe of twenty-four dancers from London in the very first show at the Royal called *Royal Revue* in September 1935. The second troupe of dancers, the Royal Rockettes, were under the direction of Ivy Bourke with costumes by de Monte and Christine Kealy. The orchestra then as in 1935 was conducted by Jimmy Campbell. Charles Wade was appointed stage and lighting director and Bob Slane was stage-manager. Stage design was in the hands of Fergus O'Farrell and Fergus O'Ryan. Apart from the fact that the whole was to be directed by Louis Elliman (or "Mr Louis" as he came to be known by his subordinates) himself, a man of equal importance, Dick Forbes, was to write the shows.

Richard Colman Forbes was born in Prince's Street, Cork, one of three sons of a master tailor. At times in the course of his stage career he was billed as Colman Forbes. During the War of Independence he joined a flying column and was captured and sentenced to 18 months in Shrewsbury Jail. On his release he went on tour with fit-up companies travelling the whole of Ireland. After his marriage to Muriel Forbes he took a job as a drummer in a band in Waterford where his daughters Pauline and Twinkle were born. In the early 1930s Dick formed a partnership with the Ennis entertainer Mike Nono and made several tours of the country with a show called *Muldoon's Picnic*. He also formed an act with Jimmy Harvey and together they made gramophone records on the Parlophone label about a character called "Mulcahy". In 1936 his play *Silver Jubilee* (which he submitted under the name "Cormac O'Daly") was placed first out of one hundred and seventeen entries, in a competition for new playwrights at the Abbey Theatre. He had also by this time written revues and sketches for the Olympia, Dublin, and the Cork Opera House. After a spell of writing for the BBC came the offer, on Noel Purcell's recommendation, to write for the Royal.

The many revues that he wrote were by general consent witty, polished and well designed to suit the talents of the resident company. The first of these, *Something in the Air*, with original music by Jimmy Campbell, appeared in 1943 and was a very fine production which ran to twelve episodes and was worthy of London's West End. There was a new script each week (the first edition ran two weeks, so amazed was the Dublin public) and set the standard for those that followed: *Variety Fair*; *Royal Review*; *Royal Spotlight*; *Royal Flush*; *Royal Parade*; *Royal Bouquet* etc. Every week the highly-trained Royalettes played a spectacular part in the success of the revues and routines like the Oriental fantasy "The Opium Dream" and the Pickwickian number "Dingley Dell" or the glittering "White Hussar" were comparable to scenes that CB Cochran, the London impresario, might have staged in one of his revues.

Each show had a different series of features: for instance, Forbes introduced potted scenes from Shakespeare in which Eddie Byrne, who had played at the Abbey and the Gate, gave a very creditable performance as Othello; Michael Ripper, who had interpreted the complete role with Lord Longford's company at the Gate, gave an excerpt from *Hamlet*, and was also seen as Shylock in the trial scene from *The Merchant of Venice*; Ginette Waddell played Catherine of Aragon in an extract from *Henry VIII*; and when Jimmy O'Dea joined the company briefly as guest star, he appeared in his famous characterisation of Bottom in *A Midsummer Night's Dream*. Also included were historical vignettes such as Robert Emmet's "Speech from the Dock" and episodes from the lives of such as Daniel O'Connell. (The latter item had to be re-cast after the first performance as the house was set on a roar when it was realised that the figure in a coach who was supposed to represent O'Connell was in fact Cecil Sheridan, the parody king, and there were enquiries from the audience to know if Cecil had his diminutive side-kick, Mickser Reid, in there with him.) Bob Hennessy, who was a wine salesman, was a tower of strength in these items and it was a matter of deep regret to Mícheál Mac Liammóir that Bob retained his semi-professional status.

But Forbes's own original comedy creations were most popular and raised Noel Purcell to star status in his own right. The weekly sketches of "Nedser and Nuala" which were written for Noel and Eddie Byrne were studies in Dublin domestic life, which could be compared in their humanity, as one critic of the period said, to the characters in O'Casey's slum plays. Eddie as the easy-going Nedser was husband to the long-suffering Nuala, played by Noel.

Their daughter, Fionnuala, was Pauline Forbes—Dick's daughter. Pauline remembers a time that her father sacked her. She overslept on the day of a dialogue rehearsal and failed to turn up on time. Her father told her that she was fired, "for keeping Mr Purcell waiting." And when she took him at his word and did not turn up again for the next day's rehearsals, she had her head eaten off all over again for keeping Mr Purcell waiting again. But she did not get fired again the second time. In the sketch, Noel used an undeniably exaggerated Dublin accent and his body movements, particularly in the use of his arms, were suited to the action. He bent his long frame and with arms weaving, stared into the face of Nedser to inform him that he was a "gurrier" (a word not then common in Dublin and one that may, in fact, have been invented by Forbes). Or Nedser might be informed that if he planned to leave the house on that evening, "he would leave it wearing a brown overcoat—with brass handles on it—I'm warnin' yeh, Byrren, I'll be dug outa yeh."

The sketches did not really give Noel the opportunity to interpret the light and shade of the character of Nuala; he put it across through sheer strength of personality which he possessed in abundance. Forbes changed the format of the sketch in 1945 when he wrote "At the Widda Duffy's" with Noel as the "Widda" and Eddie as her son "Blinker." The new arrangement did not have the appeal of the original so he reverted to "Nedser and Nuala" once more. At another stage he changed the format of the entire show, replacing the original formula with short original musicals—*Trouble in Troy; Castles in Spain; Frolics in Spring;* but, again, he reverted to the serial type show. He continued to write a single "spot" for Noel in each show and this might take the form of a comic view of characters from Irish history and legend like Conn of the Hundred Fights or Fionn MacCool. One of the most famous of these spots was a monologue in which the four seasons were personified. Here Noel abandoned the rich Dublinese which was his hallmark and gave the deeply-felt "straight" performance that the occasion demanded. Gabriel Fallon wrote in *Feature Magazine*, March 1947:

> Winter, in which Noel appears as an old Dublin granny was one of the most poignant performances I have seen on the variety stage; marking his ability for more serious work.

"March of the Seasons" by Dick Forbes

Winter

(Music..."The Last Rose of Summer")
[*Enter Noel as decrepit old woman.*]

I'm the last rose of summer left blooming alone
For all my old cronies are faded and gone;
They're up in Glasnevin or in Mount Jerome
And there's no one to show me the way to go home.

Oh! Life in its winter is dreary and chill
With only the pension my wants to fulfil
And at night in my attic, o'er my fireplace hunched,
I sigh for the past for at present I'm bunched.

The sweet blooms of friendship are withered and dead
And nothing but memories flow'r in their stead.
Oh! Cast out the petals and shatter the vase
For I am the last of the red hot ma-mas.

Ah wisha, wisha. Taw may ayusta. Seventy years deesh isn't a bad age. I mustn't grumble. I've had a good innings and a few good outings too. Seventy years of fierce struggle in the backwoods of the Coombe. I can tell you some queer skayalta of the past. D'ye know that I can remember the old coppal-trams. Old coppals was right. They were so thin that if ye stuck a lighted candle into one he'd look like a Chinese lantern. And is queen lum when the first shupa-chip opened in Dublin. Jainey, what a ha'p'orth ye got then. And I remember the horse-policemen. What smashers they were, them fellas. With their blood-stopper trousers. And their lovely waxed moustaches. Many a time I was nearly tickled to death up at the Falla Te.

And is queen lum the days of the Loopliner, when food was only three-ha'pence a pewanta. Three-ha'pence. For a rail you could bust yer stays. And they were stays in them days. None of yer bit of elastic and two suspenders. But a good strait-jacket of whalebone that kept many a colleen dass straight. Sha, straight. If ye sigged sheeus suddenly ye'd cut the thighs offa yerself. Of course we didn't call them thighs in them days. We called them gayga, and we didn't get goose-flesh exposing 'em. We kept them well covered. None of yer cad e shins scanty-panty affairs, but about catter slot yards of good flannelette. With them around ye, I'm telling ye, ye could face any winter.

Yes, and is queen lum the first railway excursion from Corkig to Kingsbridge. Blaa Cleea didn't know what is was letting itself in for then, and nobody had the wits to think of sabbytaging the train. Of course, it's too daynock anish to do anything. All the Corkmen now have squatter's rights. And is queen lum when you had to pay trasna the metal bridge. I was going trasna one day when the man said he's let me trasna free if I let him kiss me. I said alright but when I started egg lowrt Gaylig he gave me tuppence to buy bulls-eyes. I can remember some stirring times too. I remember seeing the Post Office blazing in flames....the signal fire for the new battle of freedom. I saw the country in the steel grasp of might with the Tans roaring through the streets. I saw the battle fought and won. Again I saw the Post Office arise and before it I saw our own army present arms to our own leaders. I saw me own ould Dublin in joy and sorrow; in chains and liberty and I've lived to see her in a world of chaos and

hatred, happy and at peace. Bweeakus do Yeea agus a Vawhir
Vanihe.

(Repeat the last verse and exit—to the grave?)

In this old granny, Forbes had drawn an authentic character from
the Coombe, an area reputed to have attracted many families of
Huguenots who followed the weaving trade, but it is also a fact
that many Irish-speaking families from Connemara settled there,
so it would be quite in character for this old lady to use Irish
phrases in her normal conversation.

On Sunday 24 October 1971, the first night of a week-long
centenary celebration at the Gaiety, Éamonn Andrews, the then
managing director, introduced a host of celebrities, each of whom
was asked to read or recite an extract of prose or poetry from a
favourite author. Shakespeare, Shaw, Wilde, Sheridan, Yeats and
Eliot were the choices of many. Noel Purcell selected a monologue
by a man known to few in the audience: a good friend who had
helped to mould his career thirty years previously. He was
remembering with affection an old friend and doing honour to
a name that should not be forgotten in the annals of Dublin
theatre history. The piece—reflections of an old Dublin park-
keeper which he had recited years before in *Something in the Air*
—was written by Dick Forbes, who died in August 1949, aged
only 48. A week later Noel received a letter from Éamonn Andrews:

Gaiety Theatre, Dublin
29th October 1971

My dear Noel,
You've knocked out many audiences in your time but I doubt if you've
knocked them so heavily and so happily as you did on Sunday. It was
a great Tour de Force and people are still talking about it. Many, many
thanks.

Love to you both,
Sincerely, Eamonn

When the work of Noel Purcell, the stage performer, is considered, with his song and dance routines, work in the fit-ups, revues in London, Dublin and elsewhere; as dame, Buttons and many other characters of that never-never land of pantomime, and above all as a superb monologist which gave him insights into the roles that he would play later on the legitimate stage and films, it becomes manifest that he was an outstanding personality and superb entertainer. The only other artist of similar background and comparable ability who comes readily to mind is Stanley Holloway. Noel had not wasted his time as a boy watching the greats in the Gaiety. He remembered and himself projected all their style, grace, *savoir-faire* and consummate artistry.

Working regularly fifty-two weeks of the year in the Royal for almost the duration of the war was a hard grind. In the beginning there were three shows daily but this was reduced to two. Pauline Forbes recalled: "On a Sunday when the new show was staged for the first time, everyone still had the sketches and songs of the previous week's show still in their heads. And just after they gave their first performance of the new show they would be given the scripts for the next week's show. We all had three shows in our heads at the same time, and you'd have to rehearse between the two daily performances. You ate, drank and slept the business when you played the Royal." She remembered the luxury of getting a whole four-week run in the same sketch with Noel during 1947 when one of his films, *Captain Boycott*, made up the other half of the cine-variety bill and was retained by public demand for four weeks.

Noel gave encouragement to everyone and was the acknowledged leader of the team, although he had the heaviest workload of all. Séamus Forde, who sometimes stood in for Eddie Byrne as 'Nedser' if Eddie was away filming, states that Noel was an absolute professional on the stage and a great pleasure to work with. Séamus adds, "If someone inadvertently fluffed a line or gave a wrong cue, Noel would receive an immediate apology when they came off stage. He invariably replied, 'Don't worry about it, son, you're not working with O'Dea now!'"

In addition to the weekly revues there was always a pantomime at Christmas from the pen of Dick Forbes and in which Noel always played the dame. The first Forbes panto was *Puss in Boots* (1943–4) but the most memorable of these was *Mother Goose* (1944–5), and John Finegan, the theatre critic of the *Evening Herald,* said of it:

> Beyond all doubt and argument, the greatest and most spectacular pantomime Dublin has ever seen and the like of which will hardly be seen again in anyone's lifetime, was *Mother Goose* at the Theatre Royal in 1944, marking as it did the last Christmas of World War Two. That panto established a record which has never since been equalled—it was seen by 258,000 people—one out of every three Dubliners—during its six week run. It was written by that hugely-inventive man, Dick Forbes, whose weekly shows at the Royal during the war years filled that huge theatre and gave jobs to scores, if not hundreds of Irish performers. The star of *Mother Goose* was Noel Purcell who appeared as Nuala Goose, with Eddie Byrne as Nedser Goose. Nedser and Nuala were a husband and wife couple whose hilarious domestic problems were a weekly joy at the Royal. Principal boy was Iris Lawler who had come from the Gate where she had been appearing in a play about the Brontë sisters.* The goose was played by Johnny Caross, an Austrian, who made his own costume for the role. The entire cast numbered close on eighty. The scenery for *Mother Goose* was so elaborate that part of the back wall of the Royal had to be broken down and an extension built to accommodate it. One scene, suggested by the title depicted the departure of the Wild Geese after the Treaty of Limerick, a scene beautifully mimed by the

---

* Iris married actor Aiden Grennell, and her son Nicholas Grennell is now no stranger to panto himself.

Royalettes, the famous resident troupe directed by Alice Dalgarno and Babs de Monte. Another spectacular scene had the Royalettes and the Rockettes as sailors stepping out of two enormous toy boxes to become, when they turned their backs, a battalion of soldiers. Shortly before the panto opened I met Noel Purcell. "How is it going," I asked. He replied, "It's the best panto Dick has written, it's now up to the performers." The performers came up trumps...

Jack Cruise (not yet a Royal star, but who would go on to form his own variety company later) was also in the cast. He was then employed by day as a bookkeeper in a Dublin bakery, but he had won instant success in a broadcast of an amateur panto from the Father Mathew Hall in 1936. He became known as "The Corkman from the Father Mathew Hall." Jack, complete with the largest and longest peak imaginable on his cap, created his own stage character, "John-Joe Mahockey," a yokel from Ballyslapdash-amuckery. Such was Noel's professional generosity when Cruise was second comic in the team that he often allowed him to have a much longer solo spot than it was customary for the star comedian to permit.

Another notable performer was the fine baritone Seán Mooney who played the King of Gooseland. Seán had been a printer by trade in Dollards and found himself in show business almost by chance. Noel Purcell went every Sunday to 11.30 Mass in the Star of the Sea Church, Sandymount, where he heard Seán regularly singing solo in the church choir. When Louis Elliman was searching for a singer for *Something in the Air*, Noel remembered Seán and recommended him. Seán was immediately sent for, given an audition on a Tuesday morning and by the following Sunday afternoon was on the stage for the first time in his life in the Royal—the start of a fully professional career on the stage which included an appearance in the Dublin Grand Opera Society's centenary production of *The Bohemian Girl*. The average wage

then was about £5 per week and when Seán told his father that
he was being paid £10 to sing in the Royal, his father asked him
incredulously, "Who's going to pay £10 a week to hear you sing?"
Noel, on the other hand, couldn't have been more helpful. Seán
said of him in a conversation with the author:

> Noel was a very lovable type of man. He was very straight in
> anything he did. The first Sunday I opened in the Royal I was as
> nervous as hell as I'd never been on the stage in my life. I was
> in evening dress but I knew nothing about stage make-up. Noel
> brought me into No 1 dressing room, sat me down and then he
> made me up. When he'd finished he spoke to me as one tradesman
> to another and told me that I would have to get the tools of my
> new trade. "Now son," he said, "go over to Bourkes of Dame
> Street in the morning and get sticks of five and nine greasepaint,
> carmine for your lips, black pencil for your eyebrows and powder
> to dry off your make-up. And get a needle and thread because
> you'll never know when you'll lose a button." I wasn't the only
> one he helped like that over the years, I've seen him give similar
> help to others, especially newcomers.

Seán recalled that the bigger the name in show business, the
more helpful and appreciative they were of others. On one occasion
during the run of Jimmy O'Dea's show *Let's Go* at the Gaiety,
Jimmy's singer, baritone Stephen Black, took ill and he asked
Seán, who was already doing two shows a day at the Royal, if he
would go over to the Gaiety after his second show and stand in
for Black. Seán agreed, and at the end of the show that evening
he prepared to take Black's place in the walk down in the finale
but O'Dea held him back; when it came to O'Dea's turn to walk
down last, as star of the show, he took Seán with him and
applauded him as heartily as the audience. It was a gesture of
professional generosity that Seán never forgot. He is one of the
few survivors of all those who trod the boards of the Royal and

is full of happy memories of the theatre. The audiences were
assured of value for money; for as little as a shilling up to five
o'clock they could expect to see a good feature film, a sing-along
programme with the Compton organ and when the great
showman-conductor Jimmy Campbell raised his baton to signal
the seventeen-piece orchestra, they just sat back to enjoy a first
rate stage show. Above all else the theatre itself had a friendly
ambience. Seán explained:

> We were all one big happy family—from the front of house staff,
> ushers and usherettes, the orchestra, the back-stage staff of scene
> shifters, electricians, carpenters, scene painters to the performers—
> everyone was friendly. There were no rows, no animosities. If a
> page boy came up with a message for Noel he'd get a friendly
> greeting like "What's your trouble me aul' Bunser?" ["Bunser"
> was another Purcellism.]

After Maxie Elliman's death, aged 39, he was replaced by Jack
McGrath who had been a Japanese prisoner of war and returned
to Ireland with the rank of colonel. The rigours of imprisonment
took their toll of him and he died soon after resumption of duty.
He was replaced by his assistant, James Sheil, who could be as
funny as anything that Dick Forbes might write. James (Jimmy)
had the most inconvenient habit of slipping across the road to
the Scotch House minutes before "Mr Louis" might require to see
him. This usually led to bitter recriminations from "Mr Louis"
which Jimmy listened to with suppressed glee as he shifted from
one foot to the other. On one occasion he offered "Mr Louis" the
ideal solution, ingenious in its simplicity. Louis would attach a
chain to Jimmy's ankle, this to be of sufficient length to reach
from the Royal to the Scotch House where if Jimmy felt a tug at
his ankle he would know that his presence was required and he
would return post-haste to the Royal "with his breath in his fist."
    In wartime Dublin there were shortages of everything and

most things were rationed, so the logistics of getting the shows on presented a major problem for Louis Elliman. (Noel jokingly wouldn't hear a word against Hitler: "Only for Hitler," he'd joke, "I wouldn't be anywhere—I'd probably be back at the cabinet-making.") Fabrics for costumes and canvas for the scenery were difficult to obtain. Seán Mooney was able at times to help out by some secret means, and Noel Purcell's great friend, Denis Guiney, the famous Dublin draper, was anonymously helpful. Noel would go into Clerys and his opening gambit with "Dinny" Guiney was to admire the beautifully designed glass show-cases. Guiney was of course aware that Noel had been responsible for all of these fittings. From there the conversation turned to the availability of cloth or canvas material. Perhaps "Dinny" Guiney too should be remembered for helping to keep the Royal and the Gaiety open during the war!

Louis Elliman was a sort of benign dictator; everything that received the "TR Royle" imprimatur had to be professionally first rate. He supervised everything from new orchestrations to costume designs, decided upon colour schemes in the stage lighting in order to match up scenery and costumes and of course he took rehearsals. These sometimes had their lighter moments especially if Cecil Sheridan was involved. An impatient "Mr Louis" was in the stalls one morning ready to take a rehearsal but there were no performers in sight. "Where the hell is everyone?" roars "Mr Louis" through a haze of cigar smoke. Cecil Sheridan emerged from the wings and explained that there was a newspaper photographer backstage taking photographs. "Photograph, my arse!" snorts "Mr Louis". "Wait just a minute boss and I'll see if he has a plate left," replies the retreating Cecil. The undisputed parody king, Cecil said that the secret was in introducing the minimum change to the maximum effect: Eliza's song in *My Fair Lady* became:

> All I want is a room somewhere
> Every night when I climb the stair

To realise she'll not be there
Wouldn't it be lovely!

He had a very bad stammer which disappeared completely when he went on stage. There happened to be a newspaper seller outside the Olympia who was similarly afflicted. "H-how m-much d-do I owe y-you f-for the p-papers B-Billy?" enquired Cecil. "T-he *H-Herald* e-every n-night and the *M-Mail* on T-Tuesday."

"J-Jasus C-Cecil Y-you n-nearly have me a-as b-bad as yourself," replied the frustrated newsvendor.

In 1945 Noel and Eddie played small roles in Carol Reed's *Odd Man Out* which had some curiosity value. In the first place Noel was cast as an unlikely tram conductor whose very broad Dublin accent seemed out of place in a film set in Belfast, and Reed's advisers seemed to have overlooked the fact that a Dublinman was most unlikely to be employed on the trams in Belfast at that time. Eddie Byrne actually had two speaking roles in the film and he is recognisably Eddie Byrne in both of them.

Noel was crossing Poolbeg Street one Saturday night about this time to have a drink in Mulligan's with Seán Mooney. Seán was already in there trying to make himself heard above the general noise when suddenly he fancied that he heard his name being called. He went outside and there in the middle of the road was Noel doubled up and trying to support his long frame by holding on to one ankle with one arm while the other arm clutched at his back. "What in the name of God is wrong with you, Noel?"

"I don't know, Seán, will you get me a taxi?"

Seán assisted Noel into a taxi with difficulty and brought him home to Sandymount where a worried Eileen helped Seán to get him up to the bedroom to await the arrival of the doctor. She invited Seán downstairs for a drink and as they sat chatting there was a horrific cry from upstairs. They arrived ashen-faced in the bedroom once more only to discover that Noel had managed to get out of the bed in order to say his night prayers but the difficulty was that he couldn't get back into the bed again. On the following morning Seán reported the matter to Maxie Elliman, explaining that Noel had a touch of lumbago. Maxie was devastated: Sunday was the opening of a new show and without Noel what would he do, what could he do? Louis must be informed. Just as all this confusion reached its height, Noel walked into the office to enquire what all the excitement was about!

It was typical of Noel whenever he heard people complaining in the dressing rooms about real or imagined setbacks, that he invariably commented, "What the hell are you complaining about, you're working aren't you?" He went on stage that Sunday afternoon to perform one of his most exacting routines, "Sir Roger de Coverley" complete with a high kicking soft-shoe dance. He looked really elegant in a russet tail coat and cream breeches with brown boots and top hat reminiscent of the advertisements for Johnny Walker whiskey.

Sir Roger de Coverley

Oh! Sir Roger, Roger de Coverley, Oh! Sir Roger de Coverley,
Oh! Sir Roger, Roger de Coverley, he was a bit of a lad.
Oh! Sir Roger's a bit of a lad, Oh! Sir Roger de Coverley,
My mother said I never should play with Sir Roger in the wood.
Take Sir Roger's partner's case, what a pretty damsel
She'll come back and hide her face—Pop goes the weasel.
Sir Roger is a bad lad and so say all of us.
Where are you going to my pretty maid?
I'm meeting Sir Roger
And I'm not afraid.
Do be careful my pretty maid. Oh! Sir Roger's a bit of a lad.

Given the prevailing circumstances, Noel had to accept the concept of cine-variety but he had reservations about it. He held the opinion that when the stage show followed a film, the film sound

track ruined it for the variety show. The audience became attuned
to the film sound track and when the live performers came on
they felt intimidated and obliged to roar in order to be heard. He
never assumed that there was a constant entity called "the
audience"—he was aware that every audience was a new one,
composed of a completely different group of people from any
other that had assembled in the past, and one could only hope
that each new element would be open to a sympathetic fusion
between audience and performers. Like all great performers, Noel
possessed magnetism and sympathy, a fact acknowledged by
Siobhán McKenna in an interview in the *Sunday Tribune* after
Noel's death:

> You had to have a huge rapport with the audience in a theatre
> the size of the Royal which would reach right to the gods.

The gods were so far from the stage that the performers looked
like animated dolls. Noel's most responsive audiences were children
and he delighted in getting thirty or forty youngsters up on stage
with him during a pantomime and encouraging them to lead the
singing of some panto song like "The Smoke goes up the Chimney":

> You push the damper in and you pull the damper out
> And the smoke goes up the chimney all the time.
> Glory, glory hallelujah; glory, glory hallelujah
> And the smoke goes up the chimney all the time.

Noel had another opportunity to work with children each Christmas week when he appeared as Santa Claus during special morning
children's matinées in the Savoy Cinema and led the community
singing to the accompaniment of the cinema organ played by
Alban Chambers or Norman Metcalfe. Gabriel Fallon described
Noel as "Dublin's Sad-eyed Santa Claus" in an article in the
Standard in January 1945:

Perhaps after all there is something in a name. For they called this Purcell "Noel"; in itself a token of a near-Christmas birthday. But there is much more to it than that. For all the parts—and they are many and varied—that go to the making of a brilliant versatility, he prefers that one which, linked to the great Feast, reaches down to the hearts of children. He loves playing—Santa Claus.

"It's the chis-el-ers," he declares, and on the ear of a Dubliner like myself the bells of Christs's and Patrick's (not to mention the Pro-Cathedral) seem to linger on the affectionate three syllables and fade away in the mellow husky tones.

"Yes, it's the chis-elers," he goes on. "They make the best audience of all."

Of course they do, just as children make the best artists of all; just as the best artists of all, despite the vicissitudes of their calling, manage to retain something of the best of the child within them.

"Ah yes, the chis-el-ers. You should hear them singing. You should her them singing as I hear them. It may be only 'Down Mexico Way'—which they sing well mind you, or 'Lay that Pistol Down', which they sing better. But it may be their abiding favourite, 'Holy Night' which they sing as if their little hearts would burst. All those young Dublin voices..."

Six feet four inches of smartly tailored, solemn-eyed comedian looked lugubriously down on me as the patient, good-natured voice trailed into contemplative silence. Was this man a sentiment-alist? I thought of EC Bentley and his scathing comments on the remark that one Damon Runyon's tough guys were, after all, just a lot of sentimentalists. "I know," said Bentley, "that in these times a favourable way of referring to a generous impulse or natural affection is to call it 'sentimentalism'; and a very nauseating sort of cant it is." Indeed, in that good sense all variety artists are sentimentalists and Noel is a variety artist and no exception. When I saw him in his dressing room at the Theatre Royal he was making up from a grease-paint box that had once belonged to Arthur Shields [Barry Fitzgerald's brother]. "Bought it at an auction," commented Noel, "just to remind me of the poor oul' Abbey." There was more criticism in his commiserative tones than in the fulminations of a wilderness of indignant young players. Then I remembered that this variety artist had played Joxer (to the great Arthur Sinclair's Jacky Boyle), a Joxer which might be described as the second-best Joxer in Ireland, a Joxer possessing the distinction of the first-best last-act fall.

But to return to this Santa Claus act. It is played under incredibly difficult circumstances. It is staged every morning a week or so before Christmas at the Savoy Cinema in O'Connell Street. Last year Noel played it in addition to three daily performances of pantomime in the Theatre Royal! Work that out for yourself and then tell me—if you dare—that variety artists get so much for so little.

"Aye, it was tough going all right," said Noel, "but it was worth it all the same. Just to see all those little faces looking up at you, lost in wonder...just to hear those chis-el-ers singing...Aye, 'Holy Night' that's their favourite. Oh yes, I was always on time for the panto...I had to be...I was shuttled to and fro in a taxi...Lunch?...got that somewhere between the dressing room and the stage...off a fork."

I watched him as he prepared for his character sketch of an old Dublin grannie written for him by that master of variety script writers, Dick Forbes. Forbes calls it "Winter" and so well he may. It is one of Purcell's finest characterisations. In it he blends the tragic with the gay, leading his audience to the cross-roads of laughter and tears and leaving them there somewhat bewildered at the unsuspected gamut of their emotions. Purcell's picture of this weary old heart cheering itself with revisiting of gay times past is one which marks him down as a master of the tragic-comic mask, that primal two-faced symbol of theatre, the royal insignia of the clown.

Many years ago there was a "lime-boy" at the Gaiety who nightly poured down carbon-arc benedictions on some of the greatest players that the legitimate stage has seen. Martin Harvey, Forbes Robertson, Edward Compton, Alexander Marsh, Gerald du Maurier, Louis Calvert, Beerbohm Tree. But for Noel Purcell, the "lime-boy", there were compensations. Watching these great players at their work was the principal one, of course. Learning fencing from Gerald Ames was another; Ames, one of the most handsome leading juveniles of his time, was also a world foils champion.

In a moment or two he is back to Santa Claus and the wondering upturned faces. "You know," said Noel, "if I had my way I'd give every poor chis-el-er in Dublin a special Santa Claus treat with a tree and presents and cakes and apples and sugar-stick!"

I believe he would. In fact, in my quietly inquisitive way, I have found out things about this seventy-six inch stretch of sad yet warm-hearted humanity that should be known only to— recording angels. The comedian who loves playing Santa Claus is himself still a chis-el-er at heart and the Dublin "lime-boy" who now stands in "star light" has not forgotten those days when he too looked with wondering eyes on Santa; when if he didn't sing "Holy Night" (it wasn't popular then) learned to troll out "See amid the Winter Snow." In that fact he holds the secret of his art and perhaps something more. I took a last look at him as he lay out-stretching a commodious arm-chair. The Dubliner who remains a chis-el-er at heart. The Yorick who sets his house in a roar—sitting there silent and solemn-eyed as the great Grimaldi must have sat when singing "The Oyster Crossed in Love." Purcell has it too—the gloom of the great clown.

Noel appeared in his last pantomime from the pen of Dick Forbes in 1945–6 as Dame Doolittle in *Jack and the Beanstalk*. When the Irish television went on air in 1962 Noel was asked why so little was seen of him on the new station. "No scriptwriters, me ould brown son," was his reply, "That's it, short and simple. There's been no one to write my scripts since Dick Forbes died. He was a tiny little fellow, as neat as a pin: soaking wet, he weighed only about eight stone, but what a brain he had and we killed him with work. He could write about anything and in beautiful English. You might say that when Dickie died, the old Theatre Royal died too."

CHAPTER FOUR

It almost seems as though 1946 was to be the beginning of Noel's reward for all the hard work he had done during the war years in bringing some laughter into the lives of people living in a drab city of rationing and little except wet turf to give warmth or cook on. In June 1946, Barry Fitzgerald returned to Dublin for a holiday and Gabriel Fallon, who had worked with Fitzgerald years earlier at the Abbey, introduced Noel to one of his heroes for the first time. Fallon wrote in *Feature Magazine*, March 1947:

> If Purcell was attracted by Fitzgerald, Fitzgerald certainly liked Purcell. I introduced them on a Wednesday afternoon; I didn't get home until Thursday morning. At the time Noel was preparing for an appearance as Brennan o' the Moor in Seán O'Casey's *Red Roses for Me*. He was nervous, as always; but more particularly so since this was one of his rare incursions into "the legitimate." The first night of *Red Roses* came and with it came the bould Barry. I sat behind him in a Gaiety box determined to note his every reaction to the play as a whole, but particularly to Purcell's performance. The play opened slowly and lumbered along. Suddenly Brennan's cue came. Noel entered; spoke his first difficult speech and then it was victory, victory, all the way...

The *Evening Herald* was equally enthusiastic:

> The presentation is a triumph for Ria Mooney, who it will be remembered, also directed the current production in London. She has shaped this strange memorable play—which begins as a piece about a railway strike and later swells into a rhapsody about Dublin past and present. Great interest was taken in Noel Purcell's appearance as the street musician and rugged philosopher, Brennan o' the Moor—a role played in London by his erstwhile partner in variety, Eddie Byrne. The role, which takes one right back to the early O'Casey, might have been written for Purcell so snugly does he fit into it. The ripe humour was well conveyed—as, more surprisingly, was the pathos of the final scene.

Gabriel Fallon wrote in the *Standard*:

> Noel Purcell at the Gaiety gives a magnificent performance as Brennan o' the Moor. His speech with its rich Dublin accent of tarnished velvet, his excellent timing, his gestures and movements (what Americans call his bodily plastique) are all that the author himself could desire for the play. Purcell's performance is outstanding.

A month later, in the course of an article on the play, Fallon quoted a correspondent from Glasgow:

> The one gratifying result of my visit to the play was that I saw the unearthing of another Dublin comedic genius in Noel Purcell. He will certainly add to the greatness of Dublin and Ireland's acting traditions.

The *Irish Independent* raged:

> The snobbery of those who favour the legitimate stage makes me

cry out against the thought that Noel Purcell should waste so much of his time in Variety. Here is a grand interpreter of an O'Casey role. As Brennan o' the Moor he carried the whole play on his back.

Noel was himself fascinated by the play and was so delighted by the transformation of the city at the end of Act III that he and Séamus Forde would come down from their dressing rooms each evening to watch it and listen to the poetic dialogue:

[O'Casey's stage direction reads: *The scene has brightened, and bright and lovely colours are being brought to them by the caress of the setting sun. The houses on the far side of the river now bow to the visible world, decked in mauve and burnished bronze; and the men that have been lounging against them now stand stalwart, looking like fine bronze statues, slashed with scarlet.*]
1st Man (puzzled): Something funny musta happened, for 'clare to God I never noticed her shinin' that way before.

Noel marvelled at the way in which Philip O'Flynn (then a student at the Gaiety school and later of the Abbey Theatre) delivered this short speech and it must have expressed something emotional in himself about his beloved Dublin. He experienced one of the great moments in his life of which he was enormously proud when Lilian and Dorothy Gish visited him in his dressing room to congratulate him on his performance. He was to receive another pleasant surprise one evening in the dress-circle bar.

The dress-circle bar in the Gaiety was in those days a meeting place for the big names in the Dublin theatres. Joe Kearns, who was a personal friend of Noel and managed the bars before eventually becoming house manager of the theatre, recalls that there was always a club atmosphere about the bar. One section of it was popularly known as Poison Pen Corner and one can only guess at the scandals that were related there. Louis Elliman, the managing director, held court there in the evenings, listening to ideas for new shows, most of which he rejected, and it took not a little argument from Edwards and Mac Liammóir to convince him of the merits of a one-man show like *The Importance of Being Oscar*.

Noel recalled, "Seán O'Sullivan, the painter, you'd meet him there—I loved him—laugh—they used to dread him in the Gaiety because he was always looking for pints and you couldn't get pints in the Gaiety. So I used to have to empty a water jug and put two bottles of stout in the jug, then he'd be happy. And we had Michael Scott, the great architect—that place was like a club. Then there was Winnie Menary, she was a great pal of Mícheál Mac Liammóir and had a devastating tongue. Lots of people were in dread of her; she was a great character with a very caustic wit and you never knew what she was going to say next. Sometimes we used to nip out to the back of the dress circle where there were plate glass panels at the back of the boxes and you could walk up and down on a sort of carpeted promenade and have a look at what was happening on the stage. I remember one particular week when there was a ballet company in residence and we watched this fellow in a short little bum-freezer jacket and white ballet tights doing a *pas de deux* and Winnie came on the scene and I said to her, 'Have a look at yer man in the tights.'

'What about him?' she says and she has a look herself. She jabbed me in the ribs and said, 'Falsies! Them's falsies.' That was Winnie."

Bobby Pyke, the caricaturist who had been published in *Time* magazine, might be heard to remark upon spotting the retreating figure of Fr Cormac O'Daly in his brown monk's habit: "There he goes, the original brown son!" Fr Cormac was the spiritual director of the Catholic Stage Guild. Harry O'Donovan would be there with his wife, Eileen, who sat with half-closed eye as the smoke curled upwards from a cigarette in the corner of her mouth and attracted the attention of a passing Mícheál Mac Liammóir, who would bow elegantly and say: "Good evening, Harry, and there is wonderful Eileen, so sleepily awake!" George Formby and his wife Beryl were frequent visitors when they set up home in Foxrock and Beryl displayed no evidence of her alleged and widely publicised possessiveness over her anything but gormless husband. And Jimmy O'Dea, refusing yet another drink from a total stranger, would relate his latest experience to a few close friends. It would appear that Jimmy, after attending a funeral in Glasnevin, made the obligatory visit to the Brian Boru House at Cross Guns Bridge on the return journey from the cemetery. While he was enjoying his Dimple Haig with a few fellow mourners, his arm was grasped suddenly by a stranger from another large gathering at the back of the pub. "Excuse me, Mr O'Dea," says this interloper, "but the corpse's brother would like to buy you a drink."

Incidentally, it was rarely that well-known performers could have a quiet drink anywhere in Dublin without having drinks pressed upon them by unknown admirers, and sometimes the drink might be sent down as a *fait accompli*. The strangers rarely got a drink in return, with the result that artists like Noel Purcell, Jimmy O'Dea, Jimmy Campbell and others, got the undeserved reputation of being mean. The fact was that if they bought drinks in return for every unsolicited one, they would spend their entire week's salary on drinks for people whom they did not know and were unlikely ever to meet again. Joe Kearns recalls, "Noel was a great man for the jar. (In fact I think he even invented the term 'the jar.') But what many people don't know is that Noel himself didn't touch a drink until he was thirty-five. I remember we had him in one of the O'Casey plays in the Gaiety where he had to drink a bottle of stout. But he refused to touch it one night because his mother was in the audience and she didn't know he drank." Séamus Forde remembers that the only time he ever saw Noel Purcell lose his temper was in a situation where some "gurrier" tried to ply him with drink. Noel was quite frightening as he stood over the bar messer and, grabbing him by the collar, growled:

"Isn't it a good thing for little fuckers like you that big fuckers like me are so patient!" But according to Joe Lynch, Noel normally went to great lengths to offend no one and was always considerate.

After a performance of *Red Roses* one evening, Noel made his way to the circle bar and was immediately invited into the Elliman party which included Deborah Kerr and the film producer-director Frank Launder, who were then making Irish location scenes for *I See a Dark Stranger*, and they advised him to get an agent, the result of which was that Launder cast him in the role of the schoolteacher, McGinty, in *Captain Boycott*, which was made in Ireland and Pinewood Studios. It was a small role originally but Launder was so delighted with Noel's performance that it was extended very considerably. He continued, at intervals, to work in the Gaiety during 1946 and followed his success in *Red Roses* with another O'Casey play in July, playing Séamus Shields in *The Shadow of a Gunman*. It was given a conventional and uninspired production by Gabriel Fallon. It is a two act play and was preceded by Dick Forbes and Ria Mooney in *A Sunny Morning* by the Quintero brothers.

The O'D company were touring Britain for Tom Arnold in that year and did not do an August show or a pantomime at the Gaiety. In Horse Show week TR Royle presented Mícheál Mac Liammóir, Hilton Edwards and Noel Purcell in *...And Pastures New*, described as "Fresh Fields in Revue Entertainment" by Mícheál Mac Liammóir and Dick Forbes. Produced by Hilton Edwards, the show was inventive but a little bewildering in concept as it tried to embrace the best qualities of the Theatre Royal revues and the distinctive features of the Gate Theatre's famous Christmas shows. The eighteen scenes which featured a cast of ninety ranged from a translation from the Chinese of Kwei Chen by Mac Liammóir, and the Court scene from Puccini's *Turandot* with Renée Flynn as the Princess to Dick Forbes's characterisations of particular Dublin social classes. Noel appeared as "Cecilia Centaur," a horsey lady straight from the Horse Show and in "Spring—An Idyll" he

appeared, diaphanously attired, as a Nymph representing spring
bearing a beautifully arranged bouquet of carrots:

"Spring" by Dick Forbes

*(Curtain rises. Prologue, who has come down front, looks sardonically
at Nymphs who are dancing the "Spring Song.")*

Prologue:

Well, here's our best attempt at pulchritude

In revue-style of the semi-nude.

I will admit they could make more display

But, at the paltry price you pay? Not they! *(Exit)*

*[Girls dance off at proscenium wing, stop halfway and return swiftly
followed by Noel Purcell dressed as Nymph. The girls off on opposite
side leaving Purcell centre looking surprised. Bird Calls heard.]*

Noel:

Now seven stages marks the span

Of life for ev'ry mortal man,

But woman for some obscure reasons

Has her life marked by four seasons.

The first, of course, you know is spring,

Of which I now propose to sing.

Oh, lovely Spring! Oh month of May

Excuse me if I'm seeming gay!

Chorus: *(Air: Mendelssohn's "Spring Song")*

For I am spring. Yes, happy springtime

When the heart is free.

Spring, when ev'ry woman wants to lose her liberty.

Spring, when I go ga-ga and leave cares behind

And I throw my corset to the wind.

(Whoop:) Oooh! Now life is so appealing,

Oooh! It's just that Kruschen feeling.

Let Tarzan come along,

Or else bring on King Kong,
For I am happy Springtime when the heart is free,
Spring when ev'ry woman wants to lose her liberty,
Spring when I go ga-ga and leave cares behind,
And people say that I'm gone with the wind.

Monologue

Spring is the season when woman awakes
To the fact that she soon will grow mellow;
There are men in battalions, but she knows her scallions;
So she sets out to capture a fellow.

It's the time when she joins up the old Perm-Club,
And tints up her hair with Peroxide.
Tho' she's but seventeen in her eyes there's no green,
And her skin is as thick as an ox-hide.

It's then that she seeks fully-fashioned in hose,
And her eyebrows she weeds like the Chinese,
And she saves up the price of that smashing fur-cape,
Only five pounds nineteen down, at Guineys.

'Tis then that she'll dance at the "Pally" at nights,
All bubbling with fun and small talk.
Prepared to keep hunting, for months at a time,
Until she has caught some poor hawk.

Then the eejit is brought home for "Mazie" to see,
And if he can please that ould eagle,
She'll allow him to stand her a few gins and limes
In exchange for a "coort" at the Regal.

Now this innocent fool isn't serious at all;
He's just having a little flirtation,
But he hasn't a chance when he's fast in her claws,
The poor buff is booked for duration.

She finds out where he works and the wages he gets
And how much of that money he spends;
And she totes him around ev'rywhere that she goes,
And she takes him to Bray for week-ends.

Oh! Then he is bunched, for the "Mazie" soon asks
If the young man's intentions are serious,
And, of course, the poor eejit declares that they are
'Gor the gerril has got him *dilairious*.

Then she dashes around the hire-purchasing shops
For the chesterfield suite and the bed,
And the bolsters and blankets and eiderdown quilt
And the exquisite hellytrope spread.

And he pays the instalments on all the damn lot
For the maiden has got him well harried
And then from the chapel on some gloomy morn
The poor divil staggers out—married.

She has won! She has won! She has captured her prey
In a hunt that was gory and grim;
She was bound to succeed, 'tis the spring of her life
Although it's the winter for him.

(*Repeat Chorus*)

The newspapers also commented favourably upon a fantasy song and dance routine called "Cinderella at the Window" which had previously been presented at the Gate, with music and lyrics by

Tyrell Pine, in which Kay Maher appeared as a day-dreaming servant girl who has a turf-man boyfriend (played by Noel) who is magically transformed into a sort of Bog of Allen Fred Astaire, dressed in a snow-white suit of evening tails. Noel was also noticed in a free adaptation of *The Taming of the Shrew*, in which he appeared as Katharina. The *Evening Mail* critic opined that the show "...is certain to rank among the most successful presentations of the mysterious TR Royle." During the Christmas season of 1946–7 the mystery man starred Noel in the panto *Babes in the Wood* at the Gaiety with script by Harry O'Donovan. The supporting cast included Harry Bailey, Jack Cruise, Patricia Fielding, Josephine O'Hagan (a lovely soprano from the Queen's), Chris Markey and the Royalettes. The *Sunday Independent* commented:

> Towering over all the cast, both physically and metaphorically, was Noel Purcell as the Dame. From his first entrance on a penny-farthing bicycle he had the audience eating out of his long bony hands.

Noel always made a point of making a hilarious first entrance in pantomime. Apart from the combined height of himself and the penny-farthing bicycle, his most memorable entrance was in *Mother Goose* in 1944–5 when he came on, all six foot four of him in a tiny little cart, drawn by a beautiful miniature pony. (It was so cold during the six-week run of the show that the pony had to be brought to the theatre each day in a taxi. Noel and the other performers of course came in by bicycle—those were the days of unavailability of petrol.)

1946 had been a good year for Noel; he had begun what was to become a distinguished film career and he had starred in four productions in the theatre where he had started as a call-boy and where six years earlier as a supporting performer he had felt obliged to leave because of a difference over a couple of pounds. He continued his association with the Gaiety in the following year, and in May 1947 he appeared as Sylvester Heegan in O'Casey's *The Silver Tassie* which was produced by Ria Mooney, assisted by Josephine Albericci (who was later responsible for presenting single performances of unusual plays on Sunday nights at the Gaiety; notable amongst these was James Joyce's *Exiles*). NPC in the *Irish Independent* in particular gave the play an excellent review:

> Once again we are introduced to a varied gallery of Dublin characters, which only O'Casey can create. Sylvester Heegan, head of the tenement household, is derivative of Fluther Good, and his playing by Noel Purcell stamps this fine comedian as a top liner of the legitimate stage.

Students from the Gaiety School of Acting (though not the then most notorious, Gainor Crist, the original of JP Donleavy's *Ginger Man*) took minor roles in *The Silver Tassie* and amongst them was a George Hill, who years later as George Roy Hill worked in Hollywood and directed films like *Hawaii*, *Thoroughly Modern Millie*, and *Butch Cassidy and the Sundance Kid* (for which he received an Academy Award nomination in 1969). Hill did not forget Noel when he returned to America, as the following letter testifies:

Kermit Bloomgarden
1545 Broadway, New York 36, NY

Dear Mr Purcell,

Enclosed is a copy of Look Homeward, Angel, *the play that George Roy Hill spoke to you about.*

We believe the part of WO Gant is just right for you and hope you feel the same way about it.

The play goes into rehearsal on October 14th and after a two week preliminary tour, will open at the Ethel Barrymore Theatre on November 28th. As time is of the essence in this matter, I would like to hear from

you as soon as possible. Would you cable your decision at my expense.
Sincerely yours,

Kermit Bloomgarden
August 24, 1957.

Noel had been cast in at least two films during that year which is the probable reason why he did not accept the offer.

The role of a Dublin tradesman seemed ready made for him so in June 1947 he played the itinerant plasterer in George Shiels's *Paul Twyning*, produced by Josephine Albericci. The press was unanimous in its praise.

> Noel Purcell in the title role is Noel Purcell at his best, a part delightfully adapted to his talent and he made the most of it. (*Irish Press*)

> The whole company kept the comedy going particularly Noel Purcell as the glib-tongued, double-crossing tramp plasterer. (*Evening Mail*)

> As Paul Twyning—in the comedy of that name—Noel Purcell is to the manner born and judging by the delight of last night's audience his every gesture, grimace and voice play has set the seal of success on his career as an actor of the legitimate stage. (*Evening Herald*)

NPC of the *Irish Independent* headlined his piece, "A triumph for Noel Purcell."

> Noel Purcell will probably remember his appearance in the name part of George Shiels' *Paul Twyning* at the Gaiety this week as the most enjoyable of his varied career. Its choice at the present stage of the Gaiety season of plays is a worthy tribute to an actor whose stature on the legitimate stage has recently, if public

approval is any guide, been growing to the proportions it had in the sphere of variety. In the role of the journeyman plasterer from Dublin who mixes politics and match-making, and a deal of mischievous cunning with his cement and turns the affairs of a Northern family topsy-turvy in the process, Purcell lives every moment of his tailor-made part and scores a major personal triumph with the audience...there was a measure of finesse and restraint which was acting on the highest plane. His picture of the drunk in the second act must be about the best thing he has done on any stage.

That final comment echoes Gabriel Fallon's reaction to Noel's portrayal of Joxer Daly six years earlier. Many critics made a point of referring to Noel's gestures on stage, and with good reason, for they could be truly graceful. There is a scene in his film *The Rising of the Moon* in which he offers Cyril Cusack a drink of poitín, but before using a mug he dusts it off on the entire length of his báinín-covered left arm; Noel makes of it a large sweeping gesture, unimportant in itself, but it is a glimpse of that elusive quality, poetry in motion.

Later in the year, the Lyric Theatre Company (director, Austin Clarke) presented Donagh MacDonagh's *Happy As Larry* at the Gaiety; Noel (as Darry Berell) and John McDarby appeared in a little-known one-act two-hander by Seán O'Casey, *The End of the Beginning*, as a curtain-raiser. The following notice from BK in the *Irish Independent* would seem to indicate that Noel triumphed in an O'Casey débâcle:

Seán O'Casey, having heard of rural Ireland and of a folk tale about an animal called a heifer, wrote something that, all other things being equal, could have been a script for Edgar Kennedy [an American film comedian who made one-reel shorts]. Lacking Mr Kennedy, the situation was saved by Noel Purcell's great cavorting power for parodying the human body. It is to be hoped that the laughers in the Gaiety audience really understood that their laughter was the result not of O'Casey's failure, but of Noel Purcell's success.

It was in any case the last opportunity to see him in a play for the next eight years. He began a life of globetrotting to make many important and some inconsequential films, though he did make occasional appearances in revue and pantomime at his beloved Theatre Royal.

CHAPTER FIVE

It is not proposed to deal at length with the majority of Noel's films, but it is necessary to examine the first three in some detail. These immediately established him as a natural film performer. So impressed were the experts at Pinewood Studios with *Captain Boycott* that they realised that Noel's future career lay in the cinema and that his days of Irish theatrical activity were over. *Captain Boycott* and *The Blue Lagoon* were made for Arthur Rank by Individual Films, the production company of Frank Launder and his co-producer, Sidney Gilliat. The third important film of the formative trilogy was Paul Rotha's *No Resting Place,* made on location in County Wicklow. The film was not made on the cheap, but producer Colin Lesslie's purpose was to make a naturalistic film in the manner of the best Italian post-war pictures. Paul Rotha, a famous pioneer documentary maker who had never directed a fictional tale with professional actors before, brought a documentary quality to the film.

Captain Boycott was adapted from Philip Rooney's novel of the same name, by a writing team which included Paul Vincent Carroll and Patrick Campbell. Set in the West of Ireland in 1880 it tells a story about injustice, eviction of tenant farmers and the eventual ostracisation of Captain Charles Boycott, the obdurate land factor for Lord Erne, whose defeat by the Land League gave the word "boycott" to the English language. Apart from the contributions of Irish writers to the script, it was claimed that out of twenty-nine acting parts, big and small, no fewer than twenty-one were played by Irish actors, all well known figures from the Dublin theatres. But none with the exception of Noel and Eddie Byrne would stay the course and build successful and sustained film careers. Noel had a great rapport with Frank Launder and used his influence to obtain small roles for old, less fortunate friends. Séamus de Búrca, whose company of costumiers, Burkes of Dame Street, Dublin, dressed the film, relates that one afternoon in Mullingar where a race scene was to be filmed the rain suddenly came down in torrents. (In fact it rained practically all of the time on location.) Two hundred people, fully made-up and costumed, made a dash for cover to a large marquee. As boredom descended as heavily as the rain, someone suggested to Noel that he might recite one of his Dickie Forbes monologues, and without hesitation he took a microphone and entertained the crowd. Everybody in the unit was mesmerised (especially the English technicians who had never seen Noel work before and stopped work to listen) and shouted for more. According to Séamus, Noel gave an astonishing performance that day, under very bizarre circumstances, and went up many degrees in the respect of the crew. Séamus de Búrca also has a vivid recollection of meeting John Ford, on whose film *The Rising of the Moon* he acted as costume adviser.

> I met John Ford in the Shelbourne in his suite. He remarked on my suit: "Why do you costumiers always dress the same?" He was a large formidable man with an eyepatch. He had a great love of Ireland; his family came from Spiddal. "You have come here to tell me what the Black and Tans wore," he growled. "You can't. I have seen them myself."

The part of Parnell in *Captain Boycott* was eventually played by the English actor Robert Donat. He made a memorable three-minute appearance giving the famous "leper-of-old" speech at Ennis. Yet a contemporary report relates that Anew McMaster, the great Irish actor-manager, was rushed by car from his home in Howth and thence by plane to Pinewood where, bearded and frock-coated, he was filmed delivering Parnell's speech beside models of the O'Connell monument and the old gas or oil streetlamps of Ennis. The filming of McMaster's scene coincided with a visit from His Eminence Cardinal Griffin on his first visit to a film set. It is fascinating to speculate whether this was coincidence or deliberately stage-managed! There has been no subsequent explanation for the omission of McMaster's performance in favour of that of Robert Donat, but it may have been realised that McMaster was at that time too old for the role, a deficiency for which his brilliant classical style of acting could not compensate.

The film received its Irish première at the Theatre Royal on 13 September 1947 and was attended by various Government, judiciary and civic officials. The stars of the film, Stewart Granger, Cecil Parker, Mervyn Johns, Kathleen Ryan, Eddie Byrne and Noel, and a contingent from the Rank Charm School, were presented on stage; all the ladies received bouquets from the Royalettes. It was a proud moment for Noel, and Royal audiences were in the happy position of being able to show their appreciation of their old favourites Noel and Eddie who, remarkably, were starring in both the cine and the variety sections of the programme. TR Royle devised a revuette, *Many Happy Returns*, in which they appeared in top hats and tails to sing an old Harry O'Donovan number—"Thank Heaven We Are Living in Rathgar." The cine-variety programme attracted capacity audiences to the huge 4000-seater theatre for four weeks.

Captain Boycott received widespread critical acclaim and Noel Purcell was high on the list of honours. The *Irish Independent* of 15 September noted:

If I single out Noel Purcell for special mention it is not solely because physically he was head and shoulders above those around him. As the schoolmaster, he fitted into the part like a glove, and he gives a grand performance that has, I am sure, opened up the way for further successes in screen work.

The *Evening Mail* of 20 September reported:

About Noel Purcell's handling of the schoolmaster part, there can, I think, be no two opinions. He lives every moment of it and presents its varying colours so easily and naturally that he must be written down now, even at this comparatively late stage in his career, as a "straight" actor of considerable range and depth. Some people thought his genuine Dublin out of place, but for my part I know no reason in the world why a Dublin man should not teach school in Mayo.

At least he wasn't conducting a tram in Belfast! The *London Evening News* noted:

And there are the usual brilliant character performances from Irish players that put the wind up more conventional actors who have to appear with them. In particular, watch and relish Noel Purcell as the schoolmaster rebel leader.

WA Wilcox wrote in the *Daily Mail*:

But it's the wry Irish humour of Eddie Byrne and Noel Purcell and their outraged sense of injustice that get my money. Make much of them.

Dilys Powell, of *The Sunday Times* thought:

There is a notable performance as a rabble-rouser by Noel Purcell.

In January 1948, Noel F Moran, the perceptive film critic of the *Sunday Independent*, listed his first ten personal awards for the previous year: Best Film was *Odd Man Out*, with *Captain Boycott* ("A picture which has probably done more than any other to establish Irish talent firmly in the film world") listed at number eight. Best Actor was James Mason (*Odd Man Out*) with FJ McCormick at number three in the same film. Noel Purcell was number eight for *Captain Boycott*.

Noel's next notable film was made in 1949, also for Launder and Gilliat. This was a screen adaptation of Dun Laoghaire writer H de Vere Stacpoole's novel *The Blue Lagoon*, a story about two young castaways, a boy and girl, who grow up together on a tropical island. Noel was cast as an old sea-salt, Paddy Buttons, who rescues the young pair from an exploding ship. Jean Simmons and Donald Houston played the young couple when they grew older.

The film was shot on the Yaswa group of the Fiji Islands, not without some difficulties. The water was undrinkable and the crew were plagued with mosquitos and hornets. Noel was required to wear a beard and he debated using a false one initially. He said, "The make-up men told me that while they could stick a beard on me every day, which would take about an hour, more than likely I would get dermatitis, and what use would a sick actor be 16,000 miles away from London, so I decided to grow my own beard and I have shaved it off for very few exceptions ever since." During shooting, Noel fell over a cliff accidentally before a stunt-man could take over to take the fall. He recalled that the only real sympathy he received for the crack on his mosquito-ravaged hand was from Jean Simmons, who stroked it gently, murmuring, "Poor old Uncle!"

Advance publicity heralded Noel's arrival in Fiji, with the result that the Bishop of Fiji, Most Rev Dr Victor Foley, got in touch with him. Dr Foley had been educated by the Marist fathers in Dundalk and he recalled Jimmy O'Dea and Noel Purcell doing

Sunday-night concerts in aid of the new church. The bishop entertained Noel royally and when he visited Ireland later on, Noel returned the compliment by inviting him to be his guest in Sandymount. Noel's son, Victor, was named after Dr Foley.

When *The Blue Lagoon* was released it was obvious that Noel had hit the jackpot once more. One critic wrote on 18 April 1949:

> As Paddy Buttons, the Irish sailor who could do no wrong in the eyes of children, but was always wrong in the eyes of men, Noel Purcell has his best screen part to date in *The Blue Lagoon* and plays it with considerable gusto. In fact without Noel Purcell, the film might be a very ordinary affair as indeed it is after he makes a greatly-to-be-deplored exit before it is half-way through. Purcell plays it in the spirit of a boy's adventure. To hear him sing "Come Back Paddy Reilly to Ballyjamesduff" to the two little castaways as they drift away from the burning ship in an open boat is a homely interlude that brings *The Blue Lagoon* very near to Dollymount strand.

Another commentator noted:

> Then, of course, there is the fact that in it Noel Purcell as a grizzled old Irish sea-salt has his best role to date and one that places him on the right road. The picture suffers from his all too early disappearance nearly half-way through.

After *The Blue Lagoon* Noel made another three or four relatively unremarkable films until he appeared as the stern policeman Guard Mannigan in *No Resting Place*. The film showed Noel in a new light as a performer, as may be gathered from the following extract from a New York reviewer:

> *No Resting Place* is an Irish tragedy, sombre and yet cut through with the brilliance of expert characterisation by Michael Gough,

Eithne Dunne and Noel Purcell. Their portrayals are almost as vivid as lightning sizzling through the dark clouds of a mountain storm. The film has impact, virility and fascination. There is an inevitability about the conclusion that moves with the certainty of the Greek classics. True, the hero is an impudent thieving Irish tinker, but his love for his unkempt wife and son gives him motive for many of his actions. On the other hand, the stern, relentless pursuit of the tinker by the humourless Guard Mannigan (Noel Purcell) has its great moments as well. Like Javert of *Les Misérables*, Guard Mannigan refuses to halt his efforts to bring a murderer to justice. He endures reprimands, spurns bribes, endangers his health and his life in order that the jeering tinker, who killed a gamekeeper, may answer for the murder. This picture is not a happy one...It is a black tragedy except for the dour man who demands and obtains punishment for the accidental death of the gamekeeper.

"People said I was crazy to cast Purcell for a straight part," said the film's director, Paul Rotha. "But he is a great actor as well as being a great comedian."

These films set the seal on Noel's future film career. He was constantly in demand but he was an inveterate worrier and was always uneasy until he got a call for a new film. He remained a conscientious family man with a need to provide for his wife and children. At that time he had three sons. Michael was born in May 1942 and his one and only stage appearance was in a production of *The Pirates of Penzance* at Newbridge College in 1958. Later he worked at Elstree and Ardmore and is now freelance. He is married with two daughters, Tiffany and Zara. Glynn, who was born in May 1943, also works in television and is married to Elizabeth, the daughter of actor Lionel Jeffries (director of *The Railway Children*). They have one son, Thomas. Noel's number-three son (an enthusiastic filmgoer, he referred to his sons by number one to four, like the Chinese-Hawaiian detective, Charlie

Chan), Patrick, who due to superior brain power (according to his brothers) is now in the computer business in Australia, was born in April 1946. Patrick once had the idea of following his dad into the performing arts and auditioned for Tomás Mac Anna at the Abbey Theatre, but when he heard the salary, he abandoned the idea. The youngest son, Victor, was born in April 1953 and had the distinction of winning the international Critics Award for directing the Best Irish Short Film at the Cork Film Festival in 1978. Called *Sea-Horses*, it told the story of a day at an Irish race meeting. This was no ordinary meeting but the famous Laytown Races which are held only once a year on the sands at Laytown, County Meath. On the day itself, the course has to be built from scratch and everything from tents and stalls to bookies' stands set up—and the time of the first race depends on the tide.

Spending increasingly more time away from home on film locations, Noel would have wished to see more of his family, but he left them under Eileen's guiding hand. "The only thing he was ever concerned about," says Eileen, "and the only thing he ever said to me, was, 'Don't spoil them.'"

When Noel finished his scenes in Fiji he cabled Eileen, or "Jemmy" as he called her, to meet him in New York where he planned a break for both of them. When she arrived in New York another cable awaited her explaining that a can of film had accidentally fallen into the sea and he would be delayed re-shooting some scenes. Luckily, the Purcells had friends, Kit and Jenny Reddy, in New York. Jenny had returned to Ireland in order to buy a house but Kit was living in a small apartment in 53rd Street, Manhattan, and he fixed Eileen up in a hotel in Madison Avenue which was not far from the Waldorf Astoria. She had breakfast there every morning and during the day if she wanted some peace and quiet she had the use of Kit's apartment. One afternoon she was walking along Manhattan Avenue when she heard a voice cry out in amazement, "Eileen! Jesus no, not in the middle of New York!" It was an old friend from the Theatre

Pierce Purcell, Noel's father (seated third from left)

Summer cruise SS *Homeric*, 16 June 1934 including at front Jimmy O'Dea's
first wife Bernadette and Jimmy O'Dea; at back Rev Michael Allen and Noel

Catherine Hoban, Noel's mother

Noel and Eileen Marmion (later his wife)
Coliseum Theatre, London, 1930

Jimmy O'Dea and Noel in the Irish film, *Blarney*, 1938

Noel with the famous comedian Max Wall, Theatre Royal, 1939

Noel as Dame in *That's That*, Queen's Theatre, April 1942,
with theatre manager PR Gogan, Eire O'Reilly and Jimmy Harvey

Noel making up as Nuala for one of Dick Forbes's sketches
in the series "Nedser (Eddie Byrne) and Nuala"

Noel as Mother Goose in the famous 1945–6 pantomime
—the most successful ever staged in the Theatre Royal

Royal days, Norman Barrs. When Noel arrived they saw all the latest shows on Broadway before returning to his dear delightful Dublin. A few days after his return he happened to be driving along Westland Row complete with goatee beard and very deep sun tan in his vintage 1936 Dodge saloon. Waiting for the traffic lights to change, he overhead one "chiseler" saying to another, "Janey mac, would you look at that poor old nigger driving the taxi!" He was home.

CHAPTER SIX

When he was in Ireland Noel's favourite relaxation was attending race meetings, usually in the company of his great friend, Hector Grey, who was almost as well known in Dublin as Noel himself. All the trainers and the owners and the jockeys were friends of Noel and they all loved him. He was particularly friendly with Pat Taaffe, Willie Robinson and Joe and Paddy McGrath. "I am not a gambler, really," said Noel. "I never have more than a pound on a horse. But I love the sport. I just love horses in motion on the flat or over the jumps." There is a story about the time during the war when there was no public transport after 9.30 pm and most of the performers at the Royal rode bicycles, which they parked under the stage. On one particular Saturday the afternoon show was cancelled due to a lack of electricity. Noel could scarcely believe his luck and he persuaded most of the cast and some of the backstage staff to go to Leopardstown races. The Royal party set out from Hawkins Street led by Tommy Burns and his wife Polly, who were nightly patrons at the theatre, and Maxie Elliman in a horse-drawn trap. The trap was followed by Noel Purcell sitting tall on an extremely high bicycle, Eddie Byrne, Seán Mooney, Frankie Blowers, Michael Ripper, Al Sharpe and others bringing up the rear. The party was cheered by odd groups of amazed onlookers all along the entire route to the racecourse.

Hector Grey, who counted Noel amongst his greatest friends, was reputed to be a millionaire and had several fancy goods shops around the city. But he could not break the habits of his early lifetime and delighted every Sunday morning in standing on a soap box at the Halfpenny Bridge selling all sorts of knick-knacks and magic soaps from a large suitcase, all the time extolling loudly their bargain prices to the assembled crowd which congregated regularly to witness his performance. Noel had only to mention Hector's name on the stage to bring the house down—slyly, of course; it was a nice piece of free advertising for his pal! Noel said of him:

I met Hector when he was a turf adviser many years ago. He used to sell this racing information outside the race courses when he was very young and had just come over from Scotland. His name was Alexander Scott, but in order to improve the authenticity of what he was selling, he borrowed the name of a famous Australian jockey called Hector Grey. In the beginning he used it only for the race courses but later on when he became such a successful businessman and tycoon, he decided that the name was lucky for him, so Hector Grey he remained. And what a character! The stories about him are legion.

One fellow asked him, "What percentage do you work on?"

"One per cent," says Hector.

"One per cent? Guinnesses couldn't work on one per cent."

"Well, I do," says Hector. "I buy an article for a shilling and I sell it for two!"

That was as near as Hector ever got to percentages or mathematics. Don't ever try to do Hector or you'll be second, but if you have a good story about your charity, he'll be the first to contribute a big amount. He goes out to the Chinese in Hong Kong and Tai Pan and other places due East; I met him once in Hong Kong and it was very funny to hear him doing business with a Chinese businessman from whom he was buying his novelties, bric-à-brac and ashtrays. They were arguing about a shilling a gross and things like CIF and FOB. When you are an idiot all you can do is listen, but I discovered later that CIF means carriage, insurance and freight and FOB means free on board. There's always people about who can educate you. We used to go to the Grand National together with the crowd form Moore Street, including old Willie Tyrell, the butcher. On one occasion we went with the American Ambassador to the Curragh for the Sweeps Derby and the Ambassador invited us round that night to a boxing match between the stable lads in Naas. He introduced Hector and myself to the Aly Khan, who invited us all down to his house at the stud farm and we met a beautiful lady there, Tina was her name. About fourteen of us sat down to table that night. There were two turkeys and we had a great night, a very entertaining night. The Aly himself, God rest his soul, would do anything for a laugh. He enjoyed life and I must say he told some very interesting stories. Yes, you meet some strange and wonderful people with Hector.

Noel was a very strong swimmer and often went for a dip. He would take the family to Dollymount and a home movie shows Noel and the kids desperately trying to dig their car from where it is stuck in the sands as the incoming tide rolls in relentlessly. His close friends testified that he could also be a shark at snooker or poker. He rarely missed a junior rugby match at Bective Rangers ground, claiming that they were better than the senior games. On one occasion a fellow spectator remarked to Noel on the sparseness of the attendance. "Yes, said Noel, "it's a pity they clashed with the Olympic Games!" He wasn't much interested in other sports and when in the seventies he was asked by the *Evening Press* diarist, Terry O'Sullivan, what he thought about the "Dubs" winning the All-Ireland Final he replied: "Dubs? You mean a bunch of culchies from Artane and Raheny."

An old friend, Joe Kearns, sums up Noel in three words—

amusing, humble and religious. Before going into the theatrical management for which he is best remembered, Joe worked on the Enterprise express between Dublin and Belfast. Noel often met Joe when the Enterprise came into Amiens Street station and would suggest that they go to "the Meddler." This was a reference to the weekly service devoted to the Miraculous Medal held in City Quay Church. There would, of course, be a few "jars" afterwards. When Joe became house manager of the Gaiety he had to arrange the running order of the bill for occasional charity concerts on Sunday evenings. If Noel was appearing, Joe would enquire as to how much time he would allocate him, and the invariable reply would be: "You know me, Joe, nine minutes. Get on and off...before they find out." Joe continued, "I would ask him, 'How will I bill you, Noel; where will I put you on the programme?' And do you remember in those days how every theatre programme had a line at the bottom saying, 'This theatre is disinfected throughout with Jeyes Fluid'—'Put me down with the Jeyes Fluid,' Noel would always say."

On the day Noel returned home after location on *The Blue Lagoon*, Joe was moving house, and that evening Noel was helping him to lay the stair carpet. Afterwards, he and Joe decided to do what was known as "the bona-fide" at the Goat Inn. The "bona-fide" was a system in accordance with the licensing laws whereby genuine travellers after journeying four or five miles from the city were allowed to drink after normal drinking hours until midnight. When the pair arrived at the Goat, an unexpected policeman accosted them and enquired how far they had travelled and where they were from. "From the Fiji Islands," said a straight-faced Noel. They got in!

On Sunday 13 February 1949, Noel appeared in a concert at the Royal in aid of the Catholic Stage Guild which he had helped to form a few years earlier. The Guild organised fund-raising concerts and galas which attracted the support of top names in the British and Hollywood film business. This did not go unnoticed by Dr McQuaid, the Archbishop of Dublin, who instructed the guild that film stars who were divorcées or communists must not be permitted to appear in their shows. Many a Sunday morning Noel spent in committee listening to suggested film stars being rejected because of their marital history. Exasperated one morning, he advised his fellow committee members that "Yous had better make your minds up quick or you'll even be too bloody late for Lassie!" Noel himself would talk the hind legs off a donkey but as Chesterton said: "Only the very humble men talk a lot; the conceited fellows are afraid of giving the game away."

The international release of *The Blue Lagoon* resulted in the following reports which filtered back from globetrotting citizens. Adrian Pender wrote in the *Evening Herald*:

Let me tell you about a film I saw. It was *La Isla Perdida* (to you *The Blue Lagoon*) with Noel Purcell. Believe it or not (and I have a witness), whoever did the dubbing of Spanish for friend Noel managed to convey more than a hint of his Dublin accent! And with his Spanish audience he was easily the most popular character in the film.

The *Irish Independent* foreign correspondent wrote from Vienna by air mail:

Last night I went into a cinema in the Kartnerstrasse thinking to escape the rain and improve my German. The film was entitled *Die Blau Lagune*; once inside the cinema I found that it was an English film with the sound track dubbed in German. Imagine my surprise later on when the homely Dublin features of Noel Purcell appeared on the screen. When he opened his mouth, however, he spoke in the raciest Hamburg waterfront dialect! But that was nothing to my surprise when he started to sing. Here the technicians seem to have been completely foiled in their attempts to translate him into German and I laughed until the

tears came into my eyes as the strains of "Come Back, Paddy
Reilly, to Ballyjamesduff" sung in a rich Dublin baritone echoed
through the cinema. The Austrians around me were completely
unmoved and I attracted more than one astounded look by my
merriment. No doubt thousands of Irish holidaymakers would
suddenly find themselves being transported home by the
unexpected appearance of Noel on some foreign cinema screen.

In the week that the film received its Irish premiere at the Savoy
in April 1949, Noel was appearing in *Easter Cavalcade*, a revue at
the Royal in which Eddie Byrne also appeared with his quiz show
"Double or Nothing." Noel's contribution to the show was a Dick
Forbes monologue "The Man in the Street" from the Hysterical
History series featured in *Royal Bouquet* in 1944.

"The Man in the Street" by Dick Forbes

(*Music...Enter Noel in nondescript street dress, with bowler hat and
rather harassed appearance.*)

In giving you figures from Hist'ry
Such as those you've just lately seen,
I've often unravelled some myst'ry
Surrounding some King or some Queen.

But there's one great figure unmentioned
Who has flourished for years upon years,
Who has been the backbone of each nation
But who never gets limelight or cheers.

That's the Man in the Street; the Man in the Street,
The man whom every day you meet.
Just the chap who lives next door,
The image of you and millions more.

Where'e'r you go you'll find him there
Quietly trying to do his share;
Hist'ry has no hero to bear
That valiant man, the Man in the Street.

Of course now, you all recognise me;
I'm dressed like the rest of the bunch.
I do the same routine of work every day
With a stout and a sandwich for lunch.

I'm respectable, quiet and solid
And nobody knows of my name,
Just a plain uncomplaining poor fellow
And you folks are precisely the same.

Yes, I am your brother, your cousin, your pal
We carry our burdens together.
We vote at elections and endure the result
And we grouse at the taxes and weather.

We meet at the local for a simple old jar
And a quiet game of rings once or twice;
And we leave our affairs to the big-shots on top
And just pay when they mention the price.

We carry top-weight and we must run the course
The nation depends upon us.
There's nobody else who can do it, we're told
So we carry on without fuss.

We try to be citizens, worthy that name
Behaving as citizens should
And we hate what's unjust or what's sinful and cruel
And believe in the simple and good.

We struggle and scrape for the sake of the kids
To feed them and see them well-clad
And to give them a chance in the battle of life
A far better chance than we had.

Our purses are lean but the money is clean;
We earned it honest and straight.
There's not much to save, we must spend as we earn
But we do make the dough circulate.

We might lose a bob on a horse or a dog
But that is no reason to flout us.
For the sport's in the blood of the true Irishman
And how could the Books live without us.

We haven't much brain but we've got common sense
And we're not quite so dumb as we look
And though we're not highbrow, we know what is clean,
In a picture, a play or a book.

Our critics might say we just live for the day.
Well that is no reason for sorrow;
Today is the day for the day's joy or task
And the Lord will look after tomorrow.

We're not saints but we're there at the hour of prayer.
Our troubles a brief while to shelve
And assist at Thanksgiving to Heaven above
'Though, sometimes, it's only "short-twelve."

Nor are we great heroes, tho' none can deny
A danger we'll face unafraid;
And the Church and the State never issued a call
But we answered brigade by brigade.

So give a good cheer for the hero unknown,
That fellow you every day meet,
Who smiles as he takes all the buffets of life
The plain, simple Man in the Street.

In passing, one cannot help but compare this with the robustness of Flann O'Brien's "A Pint of Plain is Your Only Man." "The Man in the Street" with all its condescension was a product of its time. Maybe the man in the street saw himself like that and felt guilty perhaps if he didn't; at a time of rationing and wage-freezes all round it may have been politic for him to keep his head down— the days of union power were in the future.

During World War II and up till 1948 when Tommy Handley, its star performer, died, the most successful comedy series on BBC radio was *ITMA* (an acronym of the original title—*It's That Man Again*) which was scripted by Ted Kavanagh, who was also associated for a short time with Harry O'Donovan in writing Jimmy O'Dea's BBC series *Irish Half Hour. ITMA* was full of strange and wonderful characters like Colonel Chinstrap, an amiable drunk ("I don't mind if I do, sir"); Mrs Mopp, a charlady ("Shall I do you now, sir?"); Fünf, a German spy ("This is Fünf speaking") Ali-oop ("You like dirty pictures, very naughty, very rude, girl in fur coat; I go I come back"); Claud and Cecil ("It's like a thistle, Cecil—no, it's my Aunt Maud, Claude") and many more. Now, as a replacement in October 1950, Kavanagh was introducing a new series on the BBC Home Service called *The Great Gilhooly* starring Noel Purcell. Ted Kavanagh wrote in the *Radio Times* in September:

On Monday you will meet Gilhooly—the Great Gilhooly—and there is at least one thing I can promise you—you have never met anyone like him before. For that matter, neither have I. Like most comedy characters, especially radio comedy characters, he is considerably larger than life, but I hope to convey in sound a fantastic funster who, much to his own amazement, becomes a

Colossus of sport and bestrides the sporting world with a series of spectacular successes when pitted against the best athletes the nation can provide. I don't remember a comedy series based solely on sport and I remember most series since I wrote my first radio script twenty-five years ago. After all, a script writer must have a good memory or how could he revive all the old gags week after week!. No matter how ancient the wheezes, how antiquated the quips, I believe the programme will bring to the microphone not only a new character but a new personality—the Irish comedian Noel Purcell. Perhaps it isn't strictly correct to call Noel a comedian. He is really a great character actor, a great personality, and no one was more pleased than I when those who heard the trial recording realised this without seeing him and indeed, without knowing his work in the past. How can I describe him? Over six feet tall with a leonine head, hazel eyes, an aquiline nose, a profile that must be seen to be believed and with a voice to match. Add to this an unmistakable sincerity, a great kindliness of manner, an ample supply of real Hibernian charm and you have the mixture known as Noel Purcell, alias "The Great Gilhooly." Noel is known in England principally for his character work in films: *The Blue Lagoon*; *Saints and Sinners*; *Captain Boycott* and at present he is getting soaked to the skin daily in the Wicklow Hills in *No Resting Place* directed by Paul Rotha. So much for films but what about his stage experience? Although he has toured England in the past, usually with Jimmy O'Dea, he is best known in Dublin, where he has been a comedy star for many years. For seven years he was resident comedian at the Theatre Royal and at one time or another he has appeared in every theatre in the Irish capital and in every town in Ireland that has a stage with a roof over it. He has played Dame in Pantomime followed by *Juno and the Paycock*, has danced and juggled, been a trick cyclist, a comedy roller skater and was in the running recently to play St. Peter in *Quo Vadis*.

I first saw him at work about ten years ago and was

tremendously impressed. Here indeed was a comedian who was different, an actor who obviously had unlimited possibilities, especially on the air. And yet it was only last month that I was able to bring him to the microphone in a character which will, I hope, fit him like a boxing glove.

I don't know how old he is. I can only pray that broadcasting doesn't put years on him. He is a great family man, with a wife who can't possibly be as young as she looks because she is the mother of three sons. He lives, of course, in Dublin but he would be at home anywhere and in any company. Strange as it may seem he has had very little radio experience and indeed, has never broadcast in England although he has appeared once on Television* and if I am any judge, will appear on the television screen again before very long. Yet at the trial recording he treated the microphone as familiarly as if it were an old friend.

Well, that is Noel Purcell as I know him and as you will know him soon, although I still feel that in introducing him to you I am trying to describe the indescribable. Boxing will be the first sport in which Gilhooly finds his feet; how long he will remain on them is still in doubt. You will hear him playing ice-hockey, cricket and football, speeding on the dirt-track, riding in the Grand National, swimming the Channel, playing marbles, indulging in any and every sport with unpredictable results. I have great faith in this newcomer to radio, Noel Gilhooly Purcell.

The supporting cast included Jack Train, Joe Linnane, Hugh Morton, Jean Capra, the Four Ramblers (one of whom was the young and struggling Val Doonican) and the musical director was Stanley Black. The producer was Gordon Crier. Kavanagh chose Noel for the series because he could not be compared with Tommy Handley. "It must be a different voice," he said. Noel's humble

---

* This was as Barnie in *The Call to Arms* by Denis Johnston, adapted and produced by John Glyn-Jones and transmitted from Alexandra Palace.

view was: "Succeed Tommy Handley? Me? You'll never find his equal!"

On the night of the first broadcast, Monday 2 October 1950, Noel received scores of "Good Luck" telegrams and the show appeared to receive critical approval, even from a rather tetchy prima donna in Dublin who sent Noel a telegram on the following morning: "Congratulations Noel—Margaret Burke Sheridan."

The newspapers were enthusiastic—at first. The *Daily Mail* recorded:

> Ted Kavanagh, who helped Tommy Handley to make millions of radio listeners laugh, had them laughing again last night. It was the first night of the BBC's *The Great Gilhooly* which brought back Colonel Chinstrap (Jack Train). Gilhooly, big and talkative Irishman, is persuaded to challenge anyone in sporting contests. He meets a US promoter and Jimmy Wilde, the famous "paperweight" champion. "You sure pack a wonderful wallop," says Gilhooly. "Wallop," replies the Colonel, "what a wonderful word." When Jimmy Wilde says: "My longest contest went 20 rounds," Colonel Chinstrap rejoins: "Twenty rounds. What wonderful hospitality."
>
> Gilhooly collapses when shaking hands with a boxer. There is a call for brandy. But the Colonel drinks it. Gilhooly, played by Noel Purcell, and Chinstrap were the foils in a show which ran with the quick-fire vitality of *ITMA*. Gilhooly, rambling Irish comedian with a mop of iron grey hair, was making his first broadcast in England. He said "My eighty-two year old mother listened in Dublin tonight." His wife Eileen was in the fashionable audience which also included Éamonn and Gráinne Andrews.

The *Daily Express* headline read:

> Ted's first show since *ITMA* makes a star
> "Gilhooly" the novice is great—by Robert Cannell

In thirty minutes last night a new BBC star was born. A new Ted Kavanagh series—the first since *ITMA*—was successfully launched. The star of the new show 'The Great Gilhooly' is six-foot-four Noel Purcell. He is as Irish as Killarney. He was facing the BBC microphone for the first time and acted every word of his part as "Gilhooly." It was radio's biggest first night for years. There were men in black ties and dinner jackets and ladies in evening gowns with sprays of roses. John Snagge, Head of Programmes Operations, Home Service, announced this opening edition. Snagge's microphone appearances are usually reserved for State occasions.

The *Daily Telegraph* said: "Noel Purcell's warm Irish personality should go far to brighten winter evenings."

Noel flew to London once a fortnight to do a live broadcast and record the following week's show. Unfortunately, Kavanagh's scripts did not maintain their initial promise. Soon newspapers were reporting:

New Gilhooly with a Load of Old Quips
by Peter Wildeblood

After days of toil, script-writer Ted Kavanagh and producer John Watt last night offered the radio public the new "stream-lined" version of their show—*The Great Gilhooly*. Previously, the programme depended mainly on stage-Irish for its fun. Now acting on the theory that double measure should convulse the customers, half the characters speak stage-English as well. The script is full of such old quips as:

"Remember his grammar is not his strong point."

"Then why did she marry his grandpa?"

Poor Mr Noel Purcell, star of the show, has to reply when asked if he knows Gray's Elegy: "I didn't even know he was ill." When someone suggests they should put a jerk in the show, the answer is, "We've got one already. His name is John Watt." Even the well-drilled studio audience could not make their reception of that jest sound too convincing. But they enjoyed Paula Green's singing—a new ingredient designed to stiffen the mixture. Colonel Chinstrap has one good line: "Excuse me. I'm off to have my alcohol tested for blood." But by and large it was a glum half hour. The show's signature tune is "It's a great day for the Irish." H'mm.

Noel grew increasingly distressed, not for his own sake—because he wasn't the butt of the growing criticism—but for Ted Kavanagh who wasn't really in good health. By the end of the previous June, Kavanagh hadn't eaten a bite of solid food for seventy-five days. Dieting on doctor's orders, he had lost four stone in eleven weeks. Noel practically implored the BBC chiefs to scrap the show but they assured him that all new shows require time in order to build up a regular audience. The real extent of Noel's distress may be judged from a letter that he wrote to Eileen:

Darling,

Thank you for your letter and sending invitation. The "do" was very good and I thoroughly enjoyed it. I met all sorts of people and all sympathised with me over the programme. All agreed the script was not funny and that although the show got a slating from the critics, my performance was excellent and would not harm me in any way. Right enough the papers over here give it a roasting. The Daily Mail *had a top line which read, "Gilhooly To Die" and when you read the piece under it you found they were taking it off in three weeks' time, and that it was poor Ted and not Gilhooly is the cause. There is a piece about us in practically every paper but now I just don't buy any as they only get me down. There is no sign of a picture or any other work after December 21 so darling we'll have a happy Christmas but after that something will have to happen to cheer us up. The radio panto which we did last night was quite good but I really hadn't much to do in it. Peter Brough and I became good friends—he kept on telling me how sorry he was for me and said we'd meet again in some other programme. Your letter was lovely and I read it over many times. You have great faith in me my darling, and with your help I'll fight back and really get somewhere. I'm very depressed and worried these last few days as my agent has made a "bags" of things. Ever since I finished the picture my fares over and back have not been paid. I had to point this out to him so now he is in touch with the BBC and God knows what is going to happen. Worry and more worry darling. I do hope the children are well and that they often ask about me. I had a packet from Joe, if you see him before me please thank him. Honestly child I don't even know what day it is so please excuse me if I ramble a bit. I'm coming home Saturday morning and should be in Collinstown about 11.30am. Any good news I will tell you then. God bless you, all my love, Noel.*

(The reference to "a packet from Joe" contains no mystery. During the war years and afterwards when some commodities were unavailable in Britain, Noel kept his English pals supplied through contacts on the mail boat. He sent things like sides of bacon and he kept his friends Bud Flanagan and Chesney Allen of the "Crazy Gang" supplied with Havana cigars when they couldn't obtain them in London.)

This letter is a pen picture of a very human, worried and seemingly vulnerable man; the antithesis of the familiar extrovert who greeted his friends enthusiastically and with genuine pleasure as "Me ould brown son." This phrase, incidentally, seems to be of British origin and Noel first heard it used by his mother. His particular degree of friendship might often be reflected in an abbreviated version when the greeting was merely, "Me ould brown!" The earliest reference to it that can be traced is on a Regal label gramophone record circa 1914 of a song by the cockney comedian Harry Champion called "Wotcher! My old brown son" (Regal-G, 6701).

Joe Lynch claims that Noel was an extremely humble, self-effacing man who had genuine doubts about his own worth. Jimmy O'Dea has gone on record expressing similar doubts about himself. It is probable that apart from a natural modesty, neither men fully understood the nature of the impact of their personalities on an audience; both had magnetism and the very necessary quality of sympathy, but they had never been exposed to them themselves. After years of working with a hard task-master like O'Dea, who could treat people professionally like dirt in order to achieve his comic effects, and exposure to complete strangers in Britain with whom the only bond was a love of the variety theatre, Noel was more than ready for stardom in his own right when the opportunity came at the Theatre Royal, and the acclaim of the film critics testified to his success in that medium. Nobody, especially Noel, would ever claim that he was a "great" actor in the classical mould, but he was a great personality and entertainer with a conscious knowledge of all the techniques and facets of his art at his fingertips. In matters of professionalism, Noel knew what was required of him and what was more important, how to deliver it. Sir Tyrone Guthrie explained the psychology of the rapport between the outstanding performer and his audience.

> Audiences look at actors who have some kind of magnetism. This
> is largely a matter of self-confidence on the actor's part, the belief
> that he is, in fact, worth looking at.

But Noel was always cautious, and advised newcomers, "Never believe your own billing." He had in his long career witnessed the decline of many top ranking stars due to the fickleness of the public and the critics. His maxim was that you are only as good as your last performance.

CHAPTER SEVEN

Noel was an avid filmgoer and took an interest in all aspects of film-making. He was a regular visitor to the Cork Film Festival where his friend, Dermot Breen, was the festival director. When he went to the pictures he took as many of his boys as could be persuaded to go with him. If he was in the film himself, the inevitable question was: "Do you die in this picture, Daddy?" and if such was the case nothing could persuade them to go. The reason for this appears to have been a traumatic experience that two of the boys had during a visit to one of Noel's movies. Noel had been away on location for a long spell without seeing his family. The boys obviously missed him and wondered about his whereabouts. One evening, Eileen noticed in the paper that one of Noel's films which she had missed was showing at the Fairview Grand cinema (the "cinema with the sunshine windows") and took Glynn and Victor with her to see it. The film was *The Seekers* which was about early settlers in New Zealand. The boys were delighted to see their Dad early on in the picture, but later on in the middle of a Maori uprising there were shots of Noel on top of a blazing. Then suddenly he disappeared into the flames with a huge spear through his chest. The two boys grew hysterical and screamed the cinema down, believing that here at last was the explanation for their father's long absence. Eileen had to get them home as quickly as possible and after making many desperate phone calls eventually got in touch with Noel in some obscure corner of Spain. The lads were appeased when they actually spoke to their father on the phone but they were to grow much older before they learned that the camera can lie.

On one occasion Noel took his youngest, Victor, then aged four, to a film in which he had a role. Father soon appeared and was quickly recognised by number four son. With wide eyes he looked at his father, looked back at the screen and then once again examined the figure beside him, who was noting the reaction with suppressed amusement. How, the little lad was obviously wondering, was it possible for the same man to be two places at once.

Eileen claims that Noel literally collected people: he knew what it was like to be lonely and friendless in a strange country, so he often brought home visiting stars after their show. Most performers like a big supper when the show is over, but Dublin landladies were not disposed to serve hot meals at a late hour. But there were always bacon and eggs and sausages available in the Purcell household and many a delighted foreigner was introduced to black and white pudding there for the first time.

When the Hamburg State Opera, on their first tour outside Germany after the war, appeared in the Gaiety Theatre, Noel the opera lover met the rather forlorn-looking principals, who he thought might be feeling self-conscious about nationality, in a corner of the Circle Bar after their performance of *The Barber of Seville*, and after an exchange of drinks and pleasantries invited them to supper down in Sandymount. The party included Horst Gunther, the baritone who had been a prisoner-of-war with the Russians. The camp commandant had him brought to his quarters and he was ordered to sing for the commandant's guests. As a result he was given extra rations and continued to sing when requested. He had no doubt that this ensured his survival. Sigmund Ruth the bass also had a bad experience with the Russians—they entered his apartment and deliberately broke up a piano for which he had saved for years. The third person was the soprano, Annaliese Rothenberger.

They accepted on condition that they would be excused as early as possible because they were very tired. In Sandymount, Noel regaled his new German friends with stories about the opera companies that visited the Gaiety when he was there as a boy, while a bemused Eileen put on the frying pan. After supper Sigmund idly fingered the keys on the Purcells' beautiful Bluthner piano in the drawing room. Possessed of some mad, contagious Irish impulse, the previously exhausted Germans were soon singing operatic arias, solos, duets and trios which filled the house until 3am. With the return to drab normality on the following morning, Eileen was concerned about the neighbours, being well aware that voices accustomed to filling opera houses would have no difficulty in disturbing the nocturnal peace of Sandymount, and apologised for the unaccustomed noise. Without exception they begged her to leave her windows open on the next occasion so that they could hear all the better. And there *were* other nights.

An unexpected arrival one morning was the British actor Bernard Lee. He was scheduled to shoot a film at Ardmore Studios, Bray, but arrived by some strange logic in Belfast. He travelled through the night by taxi and arrived in Bray in the early hours "tired and emotional" as the newspapers used euphemistically to put it. It was obvious that he couldn't work that day and when he asked about the whereabouts of his friend, Noel Purcell, the Ardmore people were only too happy to ring Noel and inform him that Bernard Lee was on his way to Sandymount where he arrived at eight in the morning, happily drunk, and stayed for the day, spending most of it playing the piano. The neighbours would have been delighted had it been José Iturbi.

In April of 1951 Noel was back in the Theatre Royal starring in a revue, *High Times*, which could, unintentionally, have been a description of the behaviour of A Gordon Spicer, the theatre organist. He was a notorious eccentric and a habitual drunk who was regularly sacked at least once a week by "Mr Louis." Gordon, no matter how drunk, walked with his hands behind his back so that when he inevitably keeled forwards, his face was terribly scarred but his hands were unhurt and intact for playing the organ. He was unconcerned about damage to his face as the audience only saw the back of his head. In *High Times* Noel was required to introduce a certain act which Gordon was to herald with a fanfare on the organ. One night Noel waited for the fanfare but it never came. Gordon was dead drunk and all the audience knew it from experience; it was all part of the homely joy of the place for them. Noel ad-libbed and joked desperately until finally Gordon pressed the button and the great Compton organ rose up slowly and dramatically from its pit. At the top Gordon paused, played a very loud fantastic note like a giant breaking wind and disappeared slowly into the pit again.

On the first night that the Germans bombed Belfast, Gordon was living in a house in that city rented by Tommy and Polly Burns, who were accustomed to Gordon's noisy nightly ascent of the stairs. On the night in question Polly awoke suddenly and dug Tommy in the ribs. "Did you hear a noise, Tommy; it's after waking me up."

"It's that bloody Gordon coming in again. We'll have to get rid of him," was the reply as another bomb fell a few streets away!

In *High Times* Noel appeared in a Dame role as Jack Cruise's mother Mrs Mahockey. Unfortunately, during the run of the show, Noel received an offer from Betty Box (who reputedly wouldn't make a film unless her good luck omen, Noel Purcell, was in it) to appear in *Appointment with Venus*. Venus was a pedigree cow which was to be rescued from one of the German-occupied Channel Islands. Nothing could rescue Noel from the fact that he had again to grow the beard which he had only recently discarded in order to play the dame, and fast! He started to grow the beard and tried to conceal it with heavy greasepaint. But you can't keep a good beard down (especially one that had become as famous as its wearer) and the problem became acute. In the end Mrs Mahockey was quietly buried, to be replaced by her twin brother!

In the same year Noel was featured in *Encore* (a film trilogy of short stories by Somerset Maugham) and he had the distinction of being complimented by the master himself. (Apologies here to Noel Coward!) In December, the London correspondent of the *Irish Independent* reported:

> Noel Purcell, now rehearsing pantomime in Dublin, has missed a nice compliment. Somerset Maugham, now hailed as the "grand old man of English letters" described him to me as a "wonderful type" after seeing him in the role of the ship's captain in "Winter Cruise," one of the three Maugham short stories which go to make up the film *Encore*. The veteran novelist and playwright had in fact seen for the third time a showing of *Encore* and each time he got more fun out of it.

Noel did, as reported above, appear in pantomime during the 1951–2 season. He was Mrs Crusoe in *Robinson Crusoe* at the Royal with Eddie Byrne as Captain Hook. The Queen's Theatre which had housed "The Happy Gang" (so named by Danny Cummins) was given over to the Abbey Theatre company when their own theatre had been destroyed by fire in July 1951, so some of the Queen's stalwarts were featured in the Royal panto that year—Cecil Nash, Frank Howard, Freddie Doyle and Mick Eustace. Noel was, of course, as outrageously unsuitable as usual for the role of the dame by the normally accepted requirements for the role, which made for hilarious entertainment.

The loss of the Queen's was a matter of genuine regret to many Dubliners of all classes and the number of literary and artistic luminaries who occupied the stage boxes each week would have surprised many who were inclined to look down their noses at the generally knockabout fun provided by the resident company of comics. But each member of "The Happy Gang" had to be a solo performer in his own right and appear in a single spot each week. Leader of the team was Cecil Nash who was also a script-writer and co-producer of the shows. He was a Welshman who had toured every corner of Ireland in every conceivable kind of show. This resulted in breathtaking versatility. Sometimes he would devise a double act with Mick Eustace who normally portrayed a brainless character called "Mickser" and regularly threatened the audience with the wrath of his granny. In fact, Eustace was a fine tenor, who took lessons regularly from Dr Vincent O'Brien. One of their double acts had Cecil and Mick as two tramps breaking into a well-appointed drawing room and being unable to resist the grand piano. Mick would seat himself at the keys and they would sing duets together. Jimmy Harvey and Danny Cummins were firm favourites especially when, in top hats and tails, they sang and tapped to such songs as "If you knew Susie." Such routines are considered "old hat" nowadays but they required considerable talent, grace and verve.

At the stage door of the Queen's there was, high on the wall, an ancient drawing in colour of a joint of ham. Underneath was printed the words—"Hams cured here." Cecil Sheridan, who was a permanent member of the Queen's company in his early days, seems to have taken this as a cue to attempt to cure other members of the company who offended him, a teetotaller, with their drinking habits. One of the worst offenders was Jimmy Harvey, and one evening Jimmy and Cecil were on stage together in a sketch and Jimmy missed some cues. Cecil was furious and berated Jimmy afterwards in one of the rather tacky dressing rooms. "You call yourself a drinker?" stammered Cecil heroically. "I could drink you under the table myself," he claimed rashly. "You could what?" said Harvey in disbelief. "You never took a drink in your life." The bizarre and bitter exchanges culminated in a contest in the circle bar after the show in which the highly-strung Cecil with an air of near panic matched Jimmy Harvey's consumption of whiskey, glass for glass. In the end, of course, Cecil had to be assisted home, but he demanded his usual nightly meal of fish and chips. It appeared too that he had his own special bottle of vinegar in his own "chipper." Despite all attempts the actual name of the chipper could not be extracted from him, with the result that his aides had to drag Cecil around the streets enquiring at every chip shop they encountered if they had Cecil's bottle of vinegar within. They were successful at last in a famous chipper, Angelo's in Aungier Street, where Cecil's bottle of vinegar was taken reverently from a glass shelf.

Jimmy Harvey could be a wicked prankster. On one occasion there was a ventriloquist on the bill who used two large dolls in his act. Jimmy placed these dolls sitting on each of the only two toilets backstage with the result that a door opened hastily appeared to reveal that the toilet was already in use.

On the morning before the final performance in the Queen's *The Irish Times* reported:

> Over 1000 people who have been lucky enough to book seats will have the bitter-sweet experience tomorrow night of being in at the end of an era—the final performance of the Queen's Theatre Company. Thousands of others will regret missing this performance. The Queen's achieved its popularity through the provision of its special brand of light-hearted humour, and just as it had this tradition, so there was a tradition among thousands of people who paid it a weekly visit. Among these regular patrons there was a genuine feeling of regret when it was announced that the theatre was to be leased by the Abbey Company until such time as it builds a new theatre of its own.
>
> Mr PR Gogan, the Dublinman who became manager and producer of the Queen's in 1937 and so successfully guided its affairs, told an Irish Times reporter last night that he could have booked every seat ten times over for the performance on Saturday. He said, "We had thousands of regular patrons—I knew seventy-

five percent of them personally—and they all seem to want to be here when we close down. The Players will be among friends when they take their last curtain call and there will be many other friends in other parts of the city regretting that they cannot be here."

Mr Gogan is proud that, although the humour at the Queen's was designed for the average Dublin family, the theatre had just as many patrons in Mount Merrion as in Crumlin or Kimmage.

The principal script writer was Ernie Murray, who was a sub-editor on a city newspaper. He was a gentle and lovable man who devoted much time to organising the annual charity football match between the Inkblots and Crackpots (Press and Stage). His sketches, some of which had a slightly dated air about them, were repeated endlessly at the Queen's, and Ernie himself admitted that some of them were inspired by the comedy he had witnessed in the old Tivoli music hall in Burgh Quay where he had worked for a time when he was a youngster as call-boy. Like Dick Forbes, Ernie Murray penned a particularly memorable and outstanding pantomime for the Queen's. This was *Aladdin*, which was produced there in the 1940s.

The theatre was demolished in 1969 and its history, like that of most old theatres, is a fascinating one. From its opening in 1829 many illustrious names appeared there; a young Henry Irving was not at all well received because he was replacing a popular local favourite; "Gentleman" Jim Corbett, the American pugilist who defeated John L Sullivan in 1892 to become world heavyweight champion, appeared there, as did Tyrone Power Senior. Arthur Lucan ("Old Mother Riley") met and married Kitty McShane when they appeared there. The great FJ McCormick made one of his first stage appearances there under his own name of Peter Judge. Cyril Cusack's step-father, Breffni O'Rourke, appeared there with Cyril's mother Moira Breffni (or Cusack) who had also appeared in the panto *Little Jack Horner* in 1916–7. And, of course,

Noel Purcell, who had a great regard for the place, made his professional debut there.

CHAPTER EIGHT

During the early fifties Noel had important featured roles in many films and slowly he was beginning to accept the reality of his worth. He was of the opinion that "there is a good living to be made in films if a man or woman contents themselves with aiming to be a sound reliable feature player; an artist's reputation for good work and reliability will soon get around and it's very seldom he'll be out of work. I was a technician, which was why I could always get work. I always knew my lines and could always hit my mark. When the film was shot, we'd see the rushes each evening and you might say to yourself, 'I don't like the way I did that,' then you find the director's quite happy with it, so in it goes. Well, that's his job so you've got to respect his judgement, but I never liked my voice, I don't know why!" What an extraordinary admission from a man whose distinctive voice was a joy for millions to listen to!

He had retained all the standards that he had acquired when he was a tradesman working with wood, and he admired the work of the film technicians. "I like to think I get on well with my fellow artists, my fellow tradesmen. I have great respect for other professionals like cameramen and lighting men. People don't realise the hours they spend setting up a scene and getting the lighting just right. Our job is very simple compared to theirs."

And Noel was notorious for spending his free time, even days off when he wasn't on call, down on the set watching other people working and noting how they got their effects.

Noel was universally acknowledged as a reliable professional in all his film work, but he wasn't overawed by the fact that he was a film star, one of the few Irish actors who worked endlessly in the medium. In fact, he wasn't averse to gently sending himself up, and in the process deflating any impression of big-headedness that he might inadvertently have given to the few knockers who were always to be found lurking around Dublin. Brendan Balfe, the well-known RTE light-entertainment presenter, recalls that he made a programme with Noel in 1977, in which Noel spoke of *Ted Laverne*, a spurious documentary about a man who never was, the mythical Ted Laverne:

Ted Laverne was a great trouper, ah, what a trouper, one of the very best. Now I remember one night after making *Moby Dick* myself and Marlon Brando (who, of course, played the role of Moby Dick) go out for a few jars with Howard Hughes and Howard says, "Why don't we all go to a theatre and see a show?" But Marlon says, "Howard, it's four o'clock in the morning. Where will we get a theatre open in Las Vegas at this hour?" Howard says, "No problem, we'll fly to London, it's only eight o'clock over there." And I say, "Well, we'll never get a flight at this hour, there are no planes." So Howard lifted the phone and bought TWA. And that's how we all ended up in London at the opening night of Ted Laverne's own musical show called *Wunderbar*. You should have heard Ted, completely self-possessed—never played in a musical before, let alone bloody write one. But you should have heard him! Was he good? He was brutal, bloody brutal!

Asked by the interviewer about the hard work involved in film-making, Noel replied: "You didn't know you were working hard, although it was a bit tougher for the ladies." Stroking his beard, he said:

> As you can see I have my make-up on me, but a lady, even a
> star, had to be in make-up at six o'clock in the morning and
> ready to be on the sound stage for filming by eight o'clock. First
> she'd have to go to the hairdresser to get the Bob Martin's Con-
> ditioning Powder in her hair, and Cherry Blossom boot-polish in
> her eyebrows, and all sorts of things like that. No, it's not easy.

His first call in 1952 was to Italy where Burt Lancaster was filming
The Crimson Pirate. After a while he decided that Eileen would
like a holiday in the sunny climate so he arranged to meet her
in Rome. Eileen happened to mention this to her friend Dr Carty,
who told her that he was planning to go to Biarritz with their
mutual friends Joe and Kathleen Brophy at that time and suggested
that she should go with them as far as Paris and they would put
her safely on the Rome Express. So Eileen stayed with them for
a short holiday in Paris before leaving for Rome where Noel booked
into the Excelsior Hotel on the Via Veneto, one of the great
hotels of Europe. The Via Veneto in those days was one of the
shrines of *la dolce vita* and it was usual to spot scores of the
beautiful and famous people seated at the sidewalk Café de Paris
while just down the street the ladies of the night paraded in
designer evening wear. Unfortunately, Noel's schedule permitted
him only one day and an evening in Rome so he gave Eileen the
choice of seeing an opera or visiting Vatican City. She chose St
Peter's and has never regretted it. They left by ferry for Ischia,
near Naples, on the following morning where Noel resumed his
role as Pablo Murphy in the film in which Burt Lancaster used all
his skills as a former trapeze artist in his swashbuckling scenes.
Lancaster became very friendly with Noel and Eileen and their
sojourn in Ischia was more like a second honeymoon than work.

The honeymoon was to continue at their next port of call,
which was in Spain, where Noel was to work on *Decameron Nights*

with Louis Jourdan, Joan Fontaine and Joan Collins. They had a week free in Madrid, whence they travelled by luxury coach to Granada. Louis Jourdan kept himself aloof and strove to appear intellectual by spending his time reading in quiet corners. Noel, who was playing a medieval monk, had some scenes with Joan Fontaine in the Alhambra. They got on very well together but Noel didn't realise how close he was one morning to disaster— he put his foot in it properly. Unaware that Joan Fontaine hadn't spoken to or about her sister Olivia de Havilland for years, he was chatting away to her one morning as usual in make-up when he enquired cheerfully: "Well, daughter, and how is your sister Olivia these days?" He was rewarded with a most polite reply. Cool, but polite.

The unit moved on to Segovia, and as Noel and Eileen were checking into their hotel they noticed a group of sympathisers around a beautiful young girl whom they hadn't seen previously and who was weeping distressfully. They gathered that she had not long been married and on her way to the film location her husband had simply disappeared in their car. A few days later the husband, dressed entirely in black shirt and slacks, complete with dark glasses (which he never removed under any circum-stances), arrived at great speed at the hotel by car and so the happy couple, Joan Collins and Maxwell Reed, were reunited.

Miss Fontaine had frequent visits from a friend who was known to the unit as Mr Nicholas. But as Noel would put it in racing parlance, the inside information was that Mr Nicholas was in reality Prince Nicholas of Greece.

Over the next several years, Noel's film commitments took him to Hollywood, Tahiti, Hong Kong, New Zealand and even the Isle of Barra in the Outer Hebrides. His friend Hector Grey would arrange his business trips to buy supplies so that he could meet Noel in Hong Kong. Whenever he returned to Dublin, Noel would be certain to make an appearance at one of the Dublin theatres. He made one of his very rare appearances at the

Capitol theatre where he delighted audiences with his Sir Roger de Coverley act and came on later in the programme dressed as a very lanky little girl with long blond tresses but with a couple of teeth missing and sang "All I want for Christmas is my two front teeth."

In 1952 he was Dame Wimple of Waffle in *Babes in the Wood* at the Royal. The *Sunday Press* critic reported:

> Theatre Royal's version of *Babes in the Wood* is the best show from Hawkins Street since the late Dick Forbes's *Mother Goose*. Additional dialogue by Tim O'Mahony, says the programme. Take a bow, Mr O'Mahony. We hope to hear more of you. Noel Purcell, as the Nurse, is back to the top of his form (all seven or eight feet of it); he even has little fragments of dances which recall his riotous ballet, "Spring Song". In Eddie Byrne, Jack Cruise and Phil Donoghue, he has a trio of double-dyed gold-plated villains to contend with.

One of the visiting acts was WH Wilkie's Chimpanzee Family, a senior member of which managed to give Noel a vicious bite— he might as well have been back in Fiji being bitten by the hornets! There was a comedy routine in the panto in which Noel as the nurse takes rejuvenation tablets in order to make herself attractive to the baron. As a part of the routine she is supposed to enter a special cabinet in which the tablet will take effect; Noel leaves the cabinet through a trick panel and when the cabinet is opened once more it reveals the diminutive Mickser Reid dressed exactly like Noel, which suggests that Noel has been allowed to regress too far. The cabinet is closed once more in order to rectify matters but when it is opened again, the cabinet contains a chimpanzee. This routine worked perfectly until Christmas Eve, when the different groups of workers, musicians and performers exchanged large quantities of drink amongst each other. The comedy team were in number one dressing room imbibing their gift of drinks from the band, and in addition to smoking (and inhaling) a huge cigar, Mickser consumed more than his share of whiskey during the course of a game of cards. He became quite belligerent and made cheeky remarks like: "Come on, come on, hurry up, it's your lead, Purcell!" This was taken good-naturedly until it was time to go on the stage for the trick cabinet routine. Noel entered and left the box, but when it was reopened there was no sign of Mickser inside. He was discovered lying inert and taken to the dressing room, where he was laid on a table. Noel expressed the opinion sorrowfully that "the poor little fellow was dead," but a visit from Dr Frank Elcock restored Mickser to his normal quicksilver movements.

Such a night could not pass without some incident involving A Gordon Spicer on the organ. He was scheduled to play a selection on the organ during the interval and took the organ as high up as it would go on its lift and, in a drunken rapture, played an endless repertoire of classical music. Pleadings, entreaties and threats from the management could not dislodge him and nobody knew where the emergency lever that would bring him down was situated. Then it was remembered that Norman Metcalfe, who played the organ at the Savoy cinema, was familiar with the Royal instrument and his assistance was immediately sought. Norman arrived after an interval looking pretty happy with himself, and not long after he went down into the organ pit Gordon slowly descended as the audience cheered loudly. There was a brief interval before the organ ascended once again and this time it was being played by Gordon and Norman in unison!

Christmas Eve at the Royal was an annual highlight in the social calendar. John Finegan, the theatre correspondent of the *Evening Herald*, said of it:

From the year that it opened—1935—the Theatre Royal in Hawkins Street was the place to be and to be found, on Christmas Eve. All active Dublin seemed to congregate in Hawkins Street as soon as darkness fell on December 24th hoping to get admission into the city's largest theatre there to meet friends who may not have been glimpsed for months, or even a year. The great theatre could not possibly hold all the would-be patrons jostling good-naturedly at the doors on Christmas Eve. Unless you were there by seven o'clock at the latest you had little hope of gaining admission.

Once inside you made a track for one or other of the two famous bars, the spacious submarine bar which ran right under the auditorium, or the smaller, elegant dress circle bar with its circular counter*. The Royal on Christmas Eve brought, in the main, a male gathering, and a young one. The drinks consumed in the bars were usually stout, by the bottle (pints were available only in the upper-circle bar). Whiskey was rarely ordered, lager was a rich chap's drink, and vodka was relatively unknown, or untasted. As the night wore on despite the rival voices coming from the stage as the artists endeavoured to make themselves heard, there would be singing in the bars. After two or three bottles of stout, "The Last Round-up," one of the favourite songs of the era, would be attempted. After four bottles, someone would try "Begin the Beguine". After six bottles voices would be raised in old-time music hall songs. Yet despite the intake of liquor, there was never rowdiness, never violence of any kind. The Christmas Eves at the Royal lasted well until the mid-1950s (with good natured chaos reigning on both sides of the curtain) until the crowds began getting unmanageable and the Royal management closed its doors on December 24th, reputedly for rehearsals.

Both Seán Mooney and Séamus Forde think that this drastic

---

* There was also a cocktail bar in this location presided over by Charles and Arthur, shaking and mixing as required.

solution was inevitable, especially as the more unruly elements in the later audiences took to throwing bottles at the performers on the stage.

CHAPTER NINE

Noel stayed at the Royal after the pantomime in January 1953 to appear in another TR Royle revue, *Royal Travelcade*, but soon he was off making films again. Between 1953 and 1955 he appeared in at least six but he came home whenever he could and his tall bearded figure continued to be a familiar sight in Dublin. People in cars waved as he passed by and startled tourists would stop in their tracks and exclaim: "Isn't that Noel Purcell the film star?" Very often he would have a quick word with them and leave them with an abiding memory of the real Dublin. More often than not he would have two or three suits draped over his arm, which he was taking to be valeted by his friends in the New York Pressing Company in Abbey Street, and from there it was only a short walk to Liffey Street, where he would have a neighbourly chat with old Jewish friends in the antique shops. It was one of the more attractive city sights to see Noel sprawled in an armchair on the pavement outside an antique shop as he chatted with the proprietor similarly seated. He was a dedicatedly peaceful man, and on the day that Lord Mountbatten was killed he was visibly shocked; he had seen it all before: World War I; the Rising; he Black and Tans; the Civil War and World War II; and he found it impossible to condone violence no matter what the motives behind it. His mother Catherine died in 1953 aged eighty-one.

He continued to support all his favourite organisations and on one occasion it was reported that an imposing bearded captain from the Merchant Navy had arrived at the fashionable Metropole Ballroom accompanied by a mermaid. They caused quite a sensation. But Noel Purcell (behind the beard) and Mrs Eileen Purcell (under the mermaid's tail and flowing wig) were delighted. "We wanted to set a good example," Noel said, "to the other people at the Variety Club of Ireland's fancy dress ball." He had borrowed the mermaid's costume which had been used by Glynis Johns as a mermaid in the film *Miranda* from the wardrobe department at Pinewood Studios.

In May 1955, Noel appeared in his last piece of legitimate theatre when he starred with Liam Redmond at the Olympia in the Illsley-McCabe production of Paul Vincent Carroll's border comedy *The Devil Came from Dublin*. Redmond was a distinguished ex-Abbey actor who found stardom in London after the war and had a number of important film roles to his credit. He had been a founder-member of the breakaway but short lived group of Abbey players known as the Players' Theatre which is remembered chiefly for its production at the Gate of Gerard Healy's famine play *The Black Stranger*, in which Arthur O'Sullivan gave the performance of his career as the harbinger of famine, Seán the Fool.

The Devil Came from Dublin was not one of Carroll's better plays, and John Finegan of the *Evening Herald* wrote:

Three fine comedy performances—by Liam Redmond, Noel Purcell and Brendan Cauldwell*—ensure a successful run for *The Devil Came from Dublin* at the Olympia.

It will certainly not rank as a major work by Paul Vincent Carroll. There are, especially in the last act, lines that have the

---

* Later of the Radio Éireann Repertory Players

Carroll hallmark for pungency, but the piece is very long in the telling (three and a quarter hours) and tumbles too frequently into broad farce. Noel Purcell, as the principal publican, whose place is the smugglers' HQ, is splendidly agile in mind and body and in his magnificent beard looks like a modern Manannán Mac Lir.

"K" in *The Irish Times* noted:

...the farce hits its highest points when it is vitalised by Noel Purcell whose exuberant scheming publican is a delight for its pacing and its pointing of lines...

This last appearance in the legitimate theatre was a matter of regret for Noel, as his great ambition was to appear with the Abbey Players in the Abbey Theatre, possibly because he felt that it would set the seal upon his reputation as a legitimate character actor. Such was his humility that he thought such an honour would be the highest accolade that the Dublin theatre world could bestow upon him.

After Noel's death, Tomás Mac Anna, an Abbey director, said:

His opening gambit whenever I met him was always—"When am I going to play in the Abbey?" On one occasion I did ask him to play in the Abbey, in O'Casey's *Red Roses for Me,* but he was busy with a film at the time. The last time I saw him was three years ago and he was sitting in a car outside the Abbey and the first thing he said to me was, "When am I going to play in the Abbey?"—we would have been very happy to have him. He would have been a great asset to the Abbey.

At the end of that year, Noel was obliged to appear clean shaven once more for his last pantomime appearance in the 1955–6 season at the Royal, which was the first panto at the theatre since

1952. TR Royle presented Noel in the name part of *Mother Goose*, and it was almost like old times. The cast included Pauline Forbes, Jack Cruise, Hal Roach (later of Jury's Cabaret fame), Frank Howard and Cecil Nash. Johnny Caross was there once again as the goose that laid the golden eggs, and Seán Mooney, Frankie Blowers and Renée Flynn led the Royal Singers. May Devitt sported an urchin-cut style hairdo as Principal Boy. *The Irish Times* critic reported:

> Film, stage and radio success has not changed Noel from what he essentially is, the typical, warm, unaffected Dublin man in the street. One of the best of all Irish pantomime dames, his power over children is one which many parents will envy, particularly at Christmas. It is this last mentioned quality which makes the scene in which little volunteer "jockeys" are called from the audience to race mechanical horses across the village green, one of the comedy highlights of the show.

Mechanical horses? Sure for Noel it wasn't work at all! Attention was also directed to the beautiful scenery designed by Michael O'Herlihy (yet another man who ended up directing films in Hollywood). His sets were described as having an Edmund Dulac quality and in themselves made *Mother Goose* worth a visit. "Mr Louis" still hadn't lost his magic touch, and his mixture of excellence was as potent as ever.

CHAPTER TEN

In 1956 John Huston made the third major movie version of *Moby Dick* in thirty years and it is by general consent the best of the three. It is the only one to come out true to Herman Melville's book. He selected the town of Youghal in County Cork which had retained a sufficiently mid-nineteenth-century appearance to make it a suitable basis for the New Bedford of 1843. After fruitless hunting in the ports of two continents Huston discovered an old square-rigger in dry dock at Dover. At a cost of more than $200,000 the ship was transformed into a replica of Captain Ahab's *Pequod*. The forty members of the cast of the all-male crew were supported by one hundred bit-part players from Youghal before filming was transferred to Fishguard. Nearly a year later the company moved to Las Palmas in the Canary Islands, where the weather was more suitable for the duckings the cast had to undergo when the whale capsizes the boats.

Noel Purcell played the ship's carpenter, but the film is memorable in Ireland because of the unusual casting of Séamus Kelly as Flask. Kelly was a familiar figure in Dublin and wrote a column in *The Irish Times* under the *nom-de-plume* Quidnunc—he was also the senior drama critic on the same paper. It is probable that a social encounter with Huston resulted in the odd piece of casting. An early accident in his cabinet-making days lent a touch of authenticity to Noel's role. He had lost his right index finger in a circular saw. "I didn't feel a thing," he recalled. "Of course, it meant I could never play the violin again—but as I'd never played it in the first place I didn't worry over much. It came in useful much later when I played the ship's carpenter in *Moby Dick*. I spent most of that picture making coffins and I was able to give a touch of realism to the part." He spent twenty-five weeks in the making of the film, appeared in many scenes and took delight afterwards in recounting that the full extent of his speaking role was five words—he was lucky, many got none at all!

In 1956 the Purcell family moved house to Sydney Parade, where they were to remain for the next five years.

When Danny Kaye played the Theatre Royal in June 1952 and gave, incidentally, a virtuoso comedy performance that is still spoken about in Dublin, he became aware of folk backstage referring to some mysterious character as "Daddy." This was, of course, the name by which Noel was affectionately known in the Royal. When Danny eventually met Noel he gazed, enthralled, at the great beard. "Oh Noel!" he exclaimed ecstatically. "Some day we will make a film together. My dad had a beard like that."

When in 1957 MGM were planning the production of *Merry Andrew*, a film with a circus background, they asked Danny Kaye whom he would have play his father in the new comedy. With that great silky silver-grey beard still vivid in his memory, Danny answered without hesitation,"You will have to send to Dublin for him." And so Noel began his long flight to Los Angeles in 1958. His bearded appearance immediately created certain mis-conceptions relating to his age (he was then fifty-seven). The film's director-choreographer Michael Kidd ordered special treatment "for this venerable old gentleman." Danny Kaye christened Noel the "Dublin Rabbi" and he acquitted himself well as Kaye's stern father who is also headmaster of a school. One critic thought that the part for the luxuriously bearded Noel was almost too straight, especially in a comedy. The *Sunday Press* of November 1959 disagreed:

> Without clowns like Danny Kaye, this sorry-for-itself world would be a much poorer place. Danny, as a teacher in a boys' school in England becomes involved with a circus and finds himself in the traditional motley of a clown. Noel Purcell has a sizeable role and, as is usual with an actor of Noel's talents, makes every word and gesture count. Several times Noel practically steals the picture from Mr Kaye.

Noel's abiding memory of that particular visit to Hollywood was his invitation to watch Danny Kaye conducting a symphony orchestra at the huge Hollywood Bowl. At one juncture Danny invited each member of the audience, on his signal, to light a match or cigarette lighter and hold it aloft. This was done on the given signal, and Noel recalled that the thousands of tiny lights in the darkness of the evening was an absolutely enchanting magical sight. Patrons of Kaye's Theatre Royal shows can recall the magical effects he obtained on a bare stage by means of stage lighting and the use of his expressive hands and arms.

"Hollywood was all right—the most religious place I ever knew," Noel recalled. "There were queues four deep for Mass every Sunday. I never noticed all the scandals that are supposed to go on in Hollywood. My companions every evening were a couple of oul' priests." This more or less bears out Jimmy O'Dea's later impressions of the place when he went there to make a film for Walt Disney. An old friend, Laurie Sherwood, who was John Huston's secretary, took Noel to the RKO studios, where Mike Todd was making *Around the World in Eighty Days*, which was literally crammed with a cast of really big names doing one-day stints in bit parts. Todd informed Noel that if MGM would release him, there was a part for him which would take only a day to shoot. It was not to be, as MGM would not oblige, and the part originally allocated to Noel was eventually played by Ronald Colman!

Father Jack O'Donnell, a personal friend of many of the really powerful in the film capital and recipient of a gift of the latest model of car each year by Louis B Mayer, showed Noel around the Paramount lot, where he met Cecil B de Mille and became a firm friend of Anthony Quinn. Someone from the Morris Agency told Noel that Fred Zinneman had him in mind for a wonderful part in *The Sundowners* should the filming of *Ben Hur* (in which Noel was provisionally cast) go off schedule. *The Sundowners* was made in 1960, in which year Noel made six films, but the latter is not listed among them. In a letter to Eileen Noel wrote:

John Ford's Irish film The Rising of the Moon *opened here last Wednesday. The critics didn't like it too well but gave me some lovely notices. George Murphy who appeared with Ronald Reagan in the Adelphi Cinema in 1947 for a Catholic Stage Guild show, came up to say "hello" and to thank me for a story that I had told on that particular show—apparently he has been dining out on it ever since. I went to Hollywood Park races where I won $12 and met Yul Brynner who is a charming fellow and we have arranged to meet again.*

John Ford invited me to his home in Bel-Air for his 38th Wedding Anniversary. He is my best press-agent; he calls me the greatest actor in Ireland—and he means it! There were only about a dozen people at the party and you would know most of them if you saw them. The best gas at the hooley was John Wayne—we sang together and danced together and got jarred together.

Another day I met Jayne Mansfield—whom you can have! I also met a grand old character on the set of Merry Andrew—*a fine opera singer in his time called Salvatore Baccaloni who plays the owner of Gallini's circus and who sings a number called "Salud" with Danny Kaye and Pier Angeli. We had many long chats about our favourite operas.*

The reference to John Wayne concealed an ambition that Noel had nurtured for most of his life. "I've always wanted to play a cowboy," he confided. "I love cowboy films. Once upon a time I used to dream that I'd play opposite 'Duke' Wayne. Then I thought I'd be happy enough just to play in any Western. A few years ago I got an offer to star in an American cowboy series for television. It came a year too late. I got a thing in my legs called neuritis which makes my knees very weak so I can't ride a horse. I had to turn the offer down." The truth, which was concealed from Noel by his family, was that the production company which planned to make a pilot for a cowboy series didn't realise that Noel was well over seventy at the time and wouldn't have been able to do it; in addition they wouldn't secure insurance because of his age.

MGM were delighted with Noel's work on *Merry Andrew* and offered him a seven-year contract, but although he loved Hollywood he loved Dublin even more. He explained:

> To me it's an affliction—loving this country! It is actually unfortunate to be born in the city of Dublin for so great is the love I have for the place I could never get out of it. This is where I was born and where I grew up. It may be a city but it only feels like a small town to me. I just wouldn't feel right living anywhere else. There was many a time when it would have been sounder economics to move closer to the meal tickets, Hollywood or London, but I could never leave this place for good. When MGM offered me the contract I said "No, I'll go home. You know where to find me if you want me again."

As Barbara McKeon has so perceptively observed, "a not uncommon trauma for many a great artist born in this celestial cesspool of a city."

Noel had already been in Hollywood for a short period to make *Lust for Life* about the artist Vincent van Gogh with Kirk

Douglas in 1955 and he returned there to complete *Mutiny on the Bounty* in 1962 and *The Story of Adrian Messenger* in 1963. During the filming of *Lust for Life* Noel was provisionally cast for the role of Balthazar in *Ben Hur*, under most unusual circumstances. Summoned to a producer's office at MGM, he poked his bearded face round the door, saw a man standing in the middle of the floor, gently practising golf swings. The man looked up. "Ever heard of Balthazar?"

"Er..." Noel hesitated.

"You're him!" snapped the producer.

Noel went off to make enquiries about this Balthazar—which might have been a football team or a racehorse for all he knew. Happily, few Hollywood producers lived up to the hardened golf-practising stereotype that Noel encountered with regard to *Ben Hur*. On his arrival in Hollywood for the first time, he received the following courteous little note:

> *Doré Schary*
> *10202 West Washington Boulevard*
> *Culver City, California*
> *October 28 1955*

Dear Noel Purcell,

We're very happy that you've joined the cast of Lust for Life *and it's nice having you here at the studio. I do hope you will enjoy your stay with us.*

Good luck and my kind regards to you.

> *Sincerely,*
> *Doré Schary*

Noel rejected other offers, notably *The Nun's Story*, Carol Reed's *Stella* and John Ford's *Gideon's Day* in anticipation of going to Rome to start work on *Ben Hur*, but there were endless delays and cancellations. At one stage the studio couldn't decide upon a suitable leading man and Noel actually arranged for a screen test for Tony O'Reilly (now Dr Tony O'Reilly the business tycoon), but O'Reilly wasn't interested and informed Noel that he had only two ambitions, to continue playing rugby and become a good lawyer. Eventually a new producer took over the film, by which time Noel was back in Dublin filming *Rooney,* and the part of Balthazar went to Finlay Currie.

On his first day in Hollywood Noel checked into the Chateau Marmont Hotel on Sunset Boulevard and he wrote to Eileen:

A lot of movie people are staying at my hotel. I walked into Sylvia Sydney this morning and you should have seen the expression on her face when she looked up at me. I had a long friendly chat with Walter Pidgeon in wardrobe this morning, everything points to my enjoying myself so all I hope is I do a good job. How are you all in Sandymount?—you're all terribly far away. There are times when I wouldn't mind changing places with Jack Plant in Moore Street.

Jack Plant was a notorious Dublin character who had scores of occupations. He might be the hind legs of a cow in a Royal pantomime; again he might be spotted parading around Dublin dressed as Charlie Chaplin and advertising Kingston's shirts. He had been in charge of the horses during the making of Olivier's *Henry V.* He got a permanent job as a cleaner in the Metropole Cinema but he took ill on one occasion and when the manager, Frank Dowling (who was himself a much-loved Dublin character and veteran of the GPO in 1916) went to visit him in his flat in Moore Street the first thing that met his eye upon entering the hallway was a very large fibre mat bearing the legend "Welcome to the Metropole." Jack was fired, and when Dowling met him some weeks later in O'Connell Street and greeted him with, "Hello Jack!" the only response was a letter from Plant which read in effect:

Kindly do not address me by my Christian name in the future as you did when I had the misfortune to meet you yesterday. I am aware that you are held in very high regard by your circle in the old pals act but to me you are the fuckin' quintessence of a bollicks.

CHAPTER ELEVEN

In February 1958, Eileen Purcell received a phone call purporting to come from a woman's weekly magazine explaining that they were planning a series of articles on the wives of well-known people. Eileen was reticent, and she said she would think about it if they would ring her back. She discussed the matter with Noel, who encouraged her to go ahead, so she made an arrangement to receive these people in her home. On the appointed morning the door-bell rang and standing on the door step were Kathleen Andrews (Éamonn Andrews' sister) and Fred O'Donovan. They seemed to be aware that Noel was not at home and revealed that they were representing *This Is Your Life* and asked for Eileen's assistance in surprising Noel. Now only that morning Eileen happened to be lighting the fire with old newspapers, and one headline that caught her eye was: "Anna Neagle cries all through *This Is Your Life!*"

"Oh my God," said Eileen. "Noel is an extremely soft hearted and sentimental man and I wouldn't put him through anything like that." They assured her that on the contrary, as the show was planned for a St Patrick's Night, it would be a carefree happy affair, starting off, for instance, with Lily Comerford's Irish dancers. Eileen explained the difficulty in getting Noel to London at all: he'd only visit it strictly on business. So the researchers got Noel's agent to ring him and talk him into going over to London to appear on Éamonn's other programme, a panel game called *What's My Line*, emphasising that it would be excellent publicity for the forthcoming release of his film *Rooney*, which he had made in Dublin with Barry Fitzgerald, John Gregson and Eddie Byrne.

Soon, the BBC producer of *This Is Your Life*, Leslie Jackson, was on the phone to Eileen.

"Is Noel in?"

"Yes, but he's going out shortly."

"Right. We can see his car from where we are down the road. Expect us when he leaves."

A bemused Eileen thought the whole business had all the ingredients of a French farce but she cooperated fully with Leslie Jackson and followed his very detailed instructions. The result was that she, as was normal, drove Noel to the airport on Friday 14 March, where she assured him that she would see him again on the following Tuesday morning, the eighteenth. Eileen dashed home and got three of her boys ready, informing them amidst great excitement what was going to happen. Victor, being too young to travel, was left in the care of Granny Marmion, an omission which he resents to this day. When Noel arrived in London, George Brown, the producer of *Rooney*, told him that Éamonn was willing to give the film a plug on *This Is Your Life* on the following Monday, St Patrick's Day, but that he would like Noel and John Gregson to be in the audience. Noel was agreeable and it was only in retrospect that he realised he was being brought to the most unusual places—lunch in rustic pubs and other locations generally outside London. He stayed at the Irish Club in Eaton Square, a secluded area of London.

Fate works in extraordinary ways. *This Is Your Life*, of which Noel would be the star, was transmitted from the old Shepherd's Bush Empire, now a BBC television centre, where twenty-eight years previously he had made his first London appearance supporting the great Jimmy O'Dea in *Irish Smiles*, in which his future wife, Eileen Marmion, was next in importance on the bill to O'Dea himself. Eileen and her boys were kept far away from the centre of London just in case they should accidentally meet Noel and, when the big night arrived, all the participants in the show were accommodated in a large dressing room at the top of the building with instructions to stay quiet. Eileen remembers telling Harry O'Donovan not to cough as Noel would certainly recognise Harry's distinctive expectorant habit.

Meanwhile Éamonn was telling Noel "confidentially" what was about to happen: Noel would be in the audience with Johnny Gregson, the show would open with the Irish dancers, and then Éamonn would say: "If there is anybody who is Irish in the audience, come on up on the stage and we'll have a bit of fun." Of course, everybody but Noel knew all about these arrangements, and when Irish people like Barbara Mullen and Lily Comerford were joined by John Gregson and George Brown, Éamonn did give a plug to the film *Rooney* and pointed out John and Noel as two of the stars.

Previously in the dressing room Noel had asked Éamonn who the subject was to be on that night and Éamonn, swearing him to secrecy, said, "It's Barry Fitzgerald. Now for God's sake don't breathe a word of it to anyone."

"Oh, never fear, Éamonn," replied Noel conspiratorially. "There'll come a moment," Éamonn continued, "when I'll talk to you about *Rooney*, then I'll say to you, 'Who's that leprechaun behind you?'—and you'll turn and say 'It's Barry Fitzgerald!'"

"Fair enough," said Noel, "everything is jake, me auld brown son."

Everything went according to plan: the dancers opened the show, the Irish were invited on stage, Éamonn spoke about *Rooney*, and then said suddenly to Noel, "Who's that leprechaun behind you?" and as Noel half turned to look, Éamonn said, "Noel Purcell, this is your life."

"Oh Christ, no!" said Noel. "It's Barry Fitzgerald."

Unfortunately, the show is not on tape as it went out in the days of live broadcasts.

One of Noel's old school teachers, Professor Caffrey, was introduced and he remembered Noel as "a good boy" (how else could he remember him on a night like that?). Harry Morrison, the lighting man from the Gaiety, who had advised Noel to train for another job so that he would always have a trade to fall back on, recalled Noel's youthful days as a call-boy and as his assistant. There were Eddie Byrne and Pauline Forbes, his old colleagues from the Royal days; Harry O'Donovan, his best man and godfather to his eldest son; and Bernadette O'Farrell, the rising young Irish star; to crown the evening, a transatlantic phone call from Danny Kaye in Hollywood, who was delighted to greet his old friend the "Dublin Rabbi." Shamrock for St Patrick's Day was presented to Noel by Mary Ryan, a little belatedly perhaps, considering the time of the evening. Of course, Eileen and the boys, Patrick, Michael and Glynn were proud to witness the popular acclaim being bestowed on Noel.

There was the usual party afterwards and Gilbert Harding, who made a career out of being professionally irritable, rang in to say it was the best *This Is Your Life* he had ever seen. The press appeared to have enjoyed it too:

> It was up to Éamonn Andrews if no one else to make last Monday night with *This Is Your Life* an Irish night on BBC television. And, sure enough, he brought us a pillar of the Irish race—all six and a half feet of bearded actor-comedian, Noel Purcell. Even that was not enough. They also brought Noel's wife and three strapping sons. Any more and it would have amounted to an invasion. A message came across the Atlantic from Danny Kaye with whom Noel Purcell has lately completed a film.
>
> *Universe* (London)

One might have guessed that Éamonn Andrews would not allow

St Patrick's Day to pass without a link with *This is Your Life*. There could not have been a happier choice than that genial Irish giant, Noel Purcell.

Yorkshire Evening Post (Leeds)

The strains of the fiddle and the steps of the Irish jig heralded in *This is Your Life* with Éamonn Andrews really at home among a broth of a crowd of boys from the Emerald Isle on the evening of St Patrick's Day. The Irishman to whom tribute was paid was the comedian and actor, Noel Purcell, but one felt that the London atmosphere rather damped the divilment which might have lighted some of the Irish eyes had the programme come from Dublin.

Bradford Telegraph and Argus

Noel Purcell told me yesterday how he was "foxed" into appearing in Éamonn Andrews' *This Is Your Life* television programme on Monday. He believed that actor, Barry Fitzgerald, was to be the subject of the programme. Until Éamonn's introductory words "Noel Purcell, this is your life," he was thoroughly enjoying the fun. Following his initial surprise, however, he reconciled himself to having his life unfolded before the eyes of an estimated ten million viewers.

Irish Independent

These excerpts, merely a selection, are an indication of Noel's widespread fame and popularity in Britain.

In March 1985, following Noel's death, a *Sunday Tribune* tribute stated:

You know the great secrecy surrounding *This Is Your Life*? Well Harry O'Donovan (who used to write the scripts for Jimmy O'Dea) was so immersed in theatre that he never watched television. While we were in Waterford on tour, Harry announced to Jimmy and Noel that "I'm just going away to do this thing for Noel Purcell, This is Your Life," and spoilt the whole thing!

The interviewee's memory, after a lapse of thirty years, must have been playing tricks. Eileen Purcell is adamant that her husband had no advance knowledge that he was to be the subject of the programme.

Noel eventually received a copy of the famous Big Red Book which is filled with many still photographs taken as the show was being transmitted.

In 1960 Noel was offered the role of Fagin in the original London production at the Albery Theatre of Lionel Bart's *Oliver*, a musical adaptation of Dickens's *Oliver Twist*. The contract was for the run of the show and Noel was reluctant to commit himself to a long run and the consequent absence from Dublin and his family. The role was subsequently played by Ron Moody, both on stage and in the film version. It was the second longest running show in London theatre history, having run for 2618 performances. He was offered the role a second time when *Oliver* transferred to Broadway and again turned it down. He also declined an offer from Sam Wanamaker to appear in a London production of O'Casey's *Purple Dust*.

CHAPTER TWELVE

Noel and Eileen moved house again in 1961 and went to live in Wilfield Road, Ballsbridge.

So far, up to that year, Noel's life had been full of incident and travel and apart from an uncertain period in the early forties, there were frequent happy intervals, especially on the sets of his many films. But in all his wanderings he would never *ever* forget *Mutiny On the Bounty*, a sentiment shared by the film's first director, Carol Reed, who abandoned his assignment when one of the film's stars, Marlon Brando, took to changing the script during shooting and showed definite signs of wanting to direct the film as well. The location scenes were shot in Tahiti, which Noel hated, and the studio work was done in Hollywood. The so-called South Sea paradise island of Tahiti was a nightmare. There were a few buildings which were called hotels there but with their raffia roofs and bamboo walls they would hardly have been so described elsewhere. And there were the nasty things in the night. The cast didn't even have mosquito nets and every night blankets were searched at bedtime for the horrible millipedes which were as big as a man's hand and could put their victims in hospital for a couple of days with a sting like the kick of a carthorse.

One morning Noel was about to plonk down on the loo, only to see a huge rat swimming about in the water, unable to climb up the porcelain. "It obviously wasn't in a very good humour," recalled Noel. "It's teeth were gnashing away like a machine gun. I have nightmares about what could have happened if I had sat down." Noel and Eddie Byrne spent their evenings sitting by an old short-wave radio trying to get one station from the hundreds that came in on the set so they could hear news of the outside world. Work on the film seemed to be jinxed. The *Bounty* had to be rebuilt, and the final cost was far in excess of the budget. The ship was fitted with engines but was only a week out from Panamá when fire broke out in the engine room. The crew were about to abandon ship when the second unit director, Jim Havens, led his men below deck in a successful life-and-death struggle with the flames. In Tahiti, Noel heard the news and waited with other members of the unit. Fire, delays and other disasters soon sent the budget creeping up to $20m. Finally, the *Bounty* hove in sight and Noel recalled: "When she did dock, she looked a great sight. Every morning we used to go on board at seven o'clock and would stay there until seven in the evening. We had our meals on board, and the ship became almost our home." Three lives were lost, and Noel witnessed one of his friends dying on an island he was growing to hate more and more.

Sometimes in the evenings, Noel and Eddie were joined by their longtime acting and drinking friend, Trevor Howard, who was playing Captain Bligh, and they would pull limes off the trees to squeeze into their gins and tonics. Food was another big problem. The diet consisted of American-style meat loaf, day after day, with the occasional dish of stewed swordfish. It had been exotic enough for the first couple of weeks but after the fourth month it was as boring as the salt pork and hardtack which helped spark off the original mutiny.

The film was a disaster. There was a running feud between Brando and Richard Harris, who kept picking rows with Brando which resulted in his wearing ear-plugs whenever Harris was about. Then, blessed relief, Harris's wife, Elizabeth, daughter of Lord

Ogmore, arrived on the island with a hamper from Fortnum and Mason's. Liz opened it up with so much care that it was generally assumed to contain the usual caviare and champagne. Instead it was a huge joint of bacon and several heads of cabbage. She cooked it that night in the proper Irish way: boiling the bacon first and then cooking the cabbage in the bacon juice. They ate it with their fingers, the succulent fat dripping down their cheeks. "It wasn't my most elegant meal," said Noel. "I suppose I have been in most of the best restaurants in the world—but it was simply the *best*."

When a deeply tanned Noel reported to make-up one morning it was decided to shave off the portion of his beard covering his upper lip and face. "I looked like a baboon's arse," he growled. Marlon Brando was genuinely concerned for Noel when his ankles became swollen and infected with insect bites. Brando became just as unhappy as everyone else. It was said that there were seven scripts for the film and nobody understood what it was all about. Brando said they had him playing a fop one moment, a sadistic beast the next, a gentleman later and a near-psychopath after that. Said one of the crew: "I've been in this business thirty years and have never seen anything like this. Lewis Milestone, the director, has fallen fast asleep in the middle of shooting. The other day he came out of his snoring and said they would shoot a certain scene and somebody had to tell him that was the scene they just finished." It was small wonder that Noel, Eddie, Trevor Howard and some of the stuntmen spent as much time as possible swimming.

Eventually the entire cast and crew were transported to Hollywood where a definite script was agreed upon. Eddie Byrne's charming wife, the actress Kitty Thuillier, had a short holiday in Hollywood before they both returned home. Noel had a few nights on the town with Broderick Crawford—"a tough man!"—and Noel was delighted when Eileen, having completed the job of changing house in Sandymount, joined him for a holiday. They lived in a hotel just opposite the studios. One of the first people that Eileen met on the set was Marlon Brando, whom she describes as a charming man. She knew that he had been concerned about Noel when he had trouble with his ankles and now she was to learn about another great Brando act of charity. "The pity is that it is only the allegedly bad things one hears about Hollywood stars," she claims. "I know for a fact that during the making of *Bounty*, Marlon took a little boy who had a deformed foot back with him to the US with the boy's grandmother and paid all hotel and specialists' expenses until the lad's foot was completely cured."

Harrison Carroll of the Los Angeles *Herald Examiner* probably anticipated the general trend when he pinpointed Noel for special mention in his review of the film on 16 November 1962:

> A truly Herculean film effort, *Mutiny on the Bounty*, premiered for charity last night at the Egyptian Theatre, offers all of the spectacle expected of it, and, undoubtedly, will be a must-see production for audiences over the entire world...Provocative also are Hugh Griffith as a leering seaman, Noel Purcell as a bearded veteran, Chips Rafferty as another lusty seaman...

Eileen had returned home and in November 1961 she received a heart-rending letter from Noel:

> *Darling,*
>
> *Can't leave the television for a moment; I am watching the terrible fire in Bel-Air. All those lovely homes and grounds up in flames, it is really terrifying. All around Stone Canyon, Bel-Air, Sepulreda all going— with schools for miles evacuated. Now the Bel-Air Hotel is being cleared of people. A third fire has broken out and all the homes in Benedict Canyon are threatened as I write. Miles and miles of fires—all those lovely homes you have seen. Now Monderville Canyon is threatened and the whole trouble is—no water! It is really terrible looking at the*

hundreds of homes going up in smoke. I am much too distressed to
answer your letter this morning, I can't get over this terrible holocaust;
all those beautiful homes, hundreds of them all in ashes. Still no word
about a finishing date but will let you know that as soon as possible.
Please excuse this but I am much too upset to say any more. You
would cry your eyes out if only you saw this terrible disaster. All those
homes gone—it's terrible.

> *Until tomorrow, darling.*
> *Noel.*

Before he came home after thirteen months' work on the film, Noel had earned £20,000, a large sum of money in those days, but when the Irish and Uncle Sam's taxmen had taken their share, he was left with only £6,000.

Back in Dublin the unimaginable was about to happen—the demolition of the Theatre Royal! The destruction of the third Theatre Royal on the same site in Hawkins Street in June 1962 was, and still seems, an act of vandalism deplored by Dubliners. No one remotely suspected that the last revue at the theatre, called, inevitably, *Royal Finale* which commenced as part of a cine-variety programme on 24 June 1962, would spell the end of an era. Cecil Sheridan's company had the sad honour of appearing in the revue and included Peggy Dell; Frankie Blowers; Mickser Reid; John Molloy; Derry O'Donovan; Alice Dalgarno, Babs de Monte and the Royalettes; Jimmy Campbell and the Theatre Royal Orchestra and the Jimmy Campbell Singers (Kay Condron, Denis Claxton, Claire Kelleher, Bill Golding and Dolores Murphy). It was a coincidence that Cecil Sheridan's show *Gossoons from Gloccamorra* was scheduled to close the famous London music hall, the Metropolitan in the Edgeware Road, but it was reprieved at the last moment and survived for a few more years. There was to be no reprieve for the Theatre Royal, and plans were finalised for the last show on Saturday 30 June 1962 at 8pm.

At the booking office tickets were sold for the last night with regular patrons getting priority—the people who had booked the same seats every Sunday night for years. There was no film on the final night; Cecil's company presented the revue and then there was an interval during which the bars were crammed to capacity. During the interval, Louis Elliman, heartbroken and dazed, wandered aimlessly around the theatre and smiled and nodded to strangers, his natural reserve shattered by extreme emotion. Up in number one dressing room, a bare, utilitarian place with cracked mirrors and dripping taps, Sheridan was telling old colleagues who were arriving in numbers to give their last contribution from the famous stage in the last part of the show, "When you close a place like this it's like digging a hole and carting away the top soil. There's nothing to fill the gap. Listen, they're in such a hurry to close places like this that one day they'll be crying out for office blocks to be turned into theatres. It's not television that's doing it, you know, it's a matter of how much more money you can make out of a square foot of property." (Cecil had a theory that the wheel always turns full circle and that people would tire of films and television and return to live shows. It was something that he would never witness himself, as he died in January 1980.)

When the final part of the show, called *Royal Cabaret*, got under way every Irish artist of note who had ever appeared in the theatre contributed his or her most nostalgic pieces. Seán Mooney sent memories flooding back to the forties with one of his best appreciated numbers, "Lilli Marlene." Josef Locke sang "Goodbye" from *The White Horse Inn*, and Peggy Dell sang "A Little Sprig of Shamrock" which she had sung on her first appearance at the Royal twenty-six years previously. (Peggy died in May 1979.)

When Noel Purcell appeared to deliver his Dickie Forbes mono-logue about the old park attendant, he was accorded a reception which was audible proof of the affection in which he was held by his old reliable audience at the Royal. Jimmy Campbell expressed in music "What I cannot say in words!"—"Now is the Hour."

Jimmy O'Dea came over from the Gaiety to speak the valediction:

> I was asked to close the Empire in Belfast; now I'm asked to close the Royal. I hope this won't become a habit, although I'm told that 160 variety theatres have closed in Britain. It was said that this was a wonderful theatre but too big; Bob Hope called it "a magnificent garage." This has been a great place where a great many people came to see a few give them enjoyment. Louis Elliman has kept it going for the past two years under great difficulties. I suppose all theatre springs from Greek drama, but when I talked to one of the ushers tonight about the closing, the word he used wasn't Greek. It might have come from *Lady Chatterley's Lover*...

The saddest man in the theatre that night was Louis Elliman, who sat with his wife Ettie in Row D of the stalls. (It is significant that the special give-away programmes printed for that night do not mention the name of "TR Royle." That name was synonymous with light, gaiety, laughter and life in the theatre—not its demise.) "We never lost money in the Royal since my family took it over," he confided, "but we saw the red light at the end of 1960. Had we carried on we would have been in trouble. As it was, the return on investment was not high enough. For instance, Shirley Bassey cost me £2,500 for a week, and apart from those high-fee stars we couldn't get reasonably good films. Even for the closing weeks we couldn't get a film to remember."

John Finegan, the theatre critic, claimed:

> The abnormally high fees demanded by visiting artists, high overheads and the coming of television were two of the factors which led the Rank Organisation to decide to demolish the theatre in favour of an office complex. Another reason was the five-week strike in May-June 1961 which was followed by another pay demand. Louis Elliman told Rank's London headquarters of the

position. Back came the message—"Close the joint."

Phil Donoghue, the theatre manager since 1954 who had been a performer there in his time, came on to the stage and thanked the audience for their enthusiasm over the years and introduced representatives of all sections of the staff, front and backstage. The cast and audience joined in singing "Auld Lang Syne," and the gold-tasselled curtain rose and fell a half dozen times on a deeply touched audience. Finally, the heavy safety curtain (known as the "iron" to theatre folks) covered with advertisements familiar to the regular patrons descended for the last time. There were no great attempts to take away souvenirs, although backstage Cecil Sheridan managed to save the key to number one dressing room and Jimmy Campbell's baton.

The time was 10.40pm.

There had been few tears on stage but a little later at a staff party, there were tears aplenty. "Mr Louis'" final command had been: "Let there be a fitting wake; let the staff and the artists drink the bars dry."

A contemporary observer wrote at the time:

> Only variety artists and members of the staff could quite appreciate
> what it meant when the Theatre Royal closed its doors forever.
> It was probably akin to having your ancestral home burnt to
> ashes or demolished to the ground. It resulted in an utterly
> different way of life for hundreds of people whose tangible
> memories had been cruelly swept away.

As the theatre emptied, many of the performers signed autographs at the stage door—Alice and Babs were there, and Seán Mooney, Frankie Blowers and the little dwarf Mickser Reid was there too. When the demolition ball went to work on Monday morning, Mickser Reid was back again—as the site tea-boy!

CHAPTER THIRTEEN

Television had attracted Noel only sporadically during his long career. In the fifties he had appeared in New York in an award-winning television production of a play by Somerset Maugham and in September 1963 he was in the prestigious Directors Company production of Ernest Kinoy's play *The Last Hangman* on NBC-TV. The executive producer-director was Fielder Cook and the play starred Ed Begley, Finlay Currie, Noel Purcell and Clive Revill. The *Daily Variety* praised the production:

> Du Pont Show of the Week
>
> *The Last Hangman* NBC-TV
>
> Du Pont's consistent quality shows in the Season opener, a well developed, in-depth dramatic episode based on the sociological effects of the Irish rebellion. Ernest Kinoy's original teleplay carefully delineates four major characters. Three are veterans of the Irish Republican Army who have spent the forty years since the rebellion intent on carrying out a "swearing" against the former Irish policemen accused of executing their compatriots. Only one is left, a retired New York subway carman. Finlay Currie, Clive Revill and Noel Purcell were superb as the aged Irishmen...

Another New York critic wrote:

> *The Last Hangman* was about as delightful an original teleplay as we've ever seen on television. Eloquently grand were Finlay Currie, Noel Purcell and Clive Revill as the three aged members of the Old Irish Republican Army who for forty years had been tracking down with murder in their eyes all the policemen responsible for the hanging of their compatriots. Splendid also as the last existing victim on their list was Ed Begley...

Noel also starred in a Yorkshire Television comedy series in 1970 called *Never Say Die* which was set in the Emmott Robinson Ward of the Victoria Memorial Hospital and featured Reginald Marsh and Wilfred Brambell (of *Steptoe and Son* fame). Noel appeared in an episode of *Dr Finlay's Casebook* and in 1975 he admitted that his last plunge in the sea was off the coast of Devon during the filming of the BBC series *The Onedin Line*. "It was a damned good series," he recalled, "until I got drowned. I remember putting to sea in an open boat with this other actor who happened to be a professional sailor. We were shooting the scene in deep water— not only did their boat take water, it also capsized!" Noel also appeared in a television series called *The Buccaneers*.

After the New York television show he travelled to Hong Kong, where he had filmed previously in 1958, to appear in *Lord Jim* with Peter O'Toole. One night he was taking O'Toole to meet an old friend of his, the head of the Hong Kong police, whom he had befriended on his previous visit, and for whom Noel used to play Santa Claus on Christmas morning in children's hospitals. Passing through their hotel lounge they paused to see what all the residents were watching on television. It was the scene in *Watch Your Stern* in which Noel, as Admiral Sir Humphrey Pettigrew, affects a most uncharacteristic plummy upper-crust British accent and attempts to make love to little Kenneth Connor who is in drag for the four-minute take. When the scene finished

O'Toole turned to Noel and said: "That was great. Who did the talking for you?" It was during the filming of *Watch Your Stern* (1960) that Noel got the first inkling that he was developing neuritis in his legs which would grow in severity over the years. He was chasing Kenneth Connor in a comedy sequence and, finding that he could not stop himself, he ran involuntarily into a shallow pond.

When he was in Hong Kong in 1958, he had arrived there from Spain where he had played Tyrone Power's father King David in *Solomon and Sheba*. In Hong Kong he was playing the ship's engineer in *Ferry to Hong Kong* which starred Orson Welles. Welles had made his stage debut at Dublin's Gate Theatre in 1932 and made a point of remarking that when Noel was earning about £20 a week in the Olympia, he himself was lucky to receive £2 10s per week from Edwards and Mac Liammóir—"When I managed to get it," he added wryly. During the shooting of the film, Noel was deeply shocked to learn about the sudden death of Tyrone Power in Spain. Noel was saddened by the tragedy since he had known and liked Power for several years but, as we shall see, he had a premonition of the tragedy. *Solomon and Sheba* was not yet completed and was to be re-filmed where necessary with Yul Brynner in the leading role, and Noel was required again for retakes. Unfortunately, Orson Welles delayed some of his scenes with Noel (according to the details of some of his recent biographies he might have been away making a private epic of his own) so he had to refuse and his role of King David was re-assigned to Finlay Currie, who it will be remembered eventually played the role of Balthazar in which Noel had originally been cast. This wasn't an unusual occurrence as both Noel and Currie frequently undertook roles that the other couldn't accept. Finlay Currie was a veteran Scottish actor with stage and music-hall experience, like Noel, and he is probably best remembered in the role of Magwitch the convict in David Lean's 1946 version of *Great Expectations*. Noel and Finlay were old friends and Currie delighted in telling Noel about the days when he appeared in the old Dublin music-hall, the Tivoli, where there was a notice displayed prominently backstage which read:

Under no circumstances will tenors be permitted to sing "Killarney."

Noel and Finlay stayed at the Algonquin Hotel in New York when they were rehearsing the television play *The Last Hangman* and they often strolled down to St Patrick's Cathedral and paid a visit. Noel's fondest memory of Currie, who died in 1968, related to a little poem that his friend had recited about the value of visits to a church. Noel unfailingly told little children about it on their First Communion days:

Now I once knew a lovely man called Finlay Currie. We were very old men at the time and we were in New York and we came out of St Patrick's Cathedral and I said to him, "I didn't know you were so religious, Finlay," and he said "I'm not too bad at it; no matter where I am I always come into a church—as a matter of fact my dear mother had a little poem about it and it goes like this:

Whenever I am near a church
I walk in for a visit;
So that when I'm carried in
The Lord won't say "Who is it?"

Noel said that of all the sermons he had heard it was the one he liked best. It has since circulated around the world.

Quite a number of theatrical folk take their religion seriously but they are not sanctimonious about it. Members of the Catholic Stage Guild made an annual daily retreat at Mount Anville convent, the principal feature of which was that the day was spent in absolute silence and meditation with rosaries and stations of the

Sean Mooney, the celebrated baritone, the only surviving
member of the cast of the Royal wartime revues

Noel as "Brennan on the Moor" in Sean O'Casey's *Red Roses for Me*,
Gaiety Theatre, June 1946

Harry O'Donovan's famous sketch, "Mrs Mulligan in the Tram,"
with from left, Jimmy Wiseman, Ina Talbot, Ray Zack, Tom Dunne,
Jimmy O'Dea and Noel Purcell

Noel with Stewart Granger and Eddie Byrne in the film *Captain Boycott*, 1947

Noel on a visit to the firm where he learned his trade of joiner

Cecil Sheridan (the "Parody King"), Mickser Reid and Noel christening a lion
cub at Buff Bill's Circus, 10 June 1956

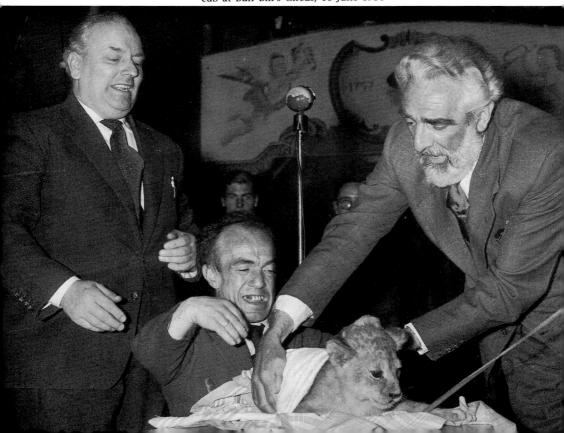

Noel, Barry Fitzgerald and John Gregson at reception in the Metropole
to publicise the film *Rooney*, 26 August 1957

Noel with Hollywood tough guy James Cagney
after filming *Shake Hands with the Devil*, 1959

Noel and Archbishop McQuaid at *The Messiah* at the Theatre Royal

Noel and Tony Kenny in *Joseph and the Amazing Technicolor Dreamcoat*,
Gaiety Theatre, 1978

Noel and Eileen's family Michael, Patrick, Victor, Glynn (clockwise from top)

Noel and his best friend, the legendary Hector Grey

Noel—Freeman of Dublin—with Maureen Potter on his left
and Eileen on his right

cross to relieve the monotony. Noel was kneeling in silence among the crowd on one particular Holy Thursday when Cecil Sheridan sidled up beside him and passed him a note. Noel opened the piece of paper surreptitiously and read, "So you won't talk, huh?" Noel broke up on the spot and that was the end of the silence for that particular year.

CHAPTER FOURTEEN

Noel continued to make films in the sixties and seventies with occasional triumphant returns to the live theatre.

Around 1965 Joseph Strick had been filming Joyce's *Ulysses* in the city, and strangely the most quintessentially Dubliner of them all does not appear in the cast list of the film, which was described by Stanley Kauffmann as "a facile and ludicrous reduction." Even more ludicrous was the fact that the script received merely an Academy Award nomination. "I remember," recalled Noel about Strick, "that the producer gave me a script and said 'pick a part...' but the book is about 1000 pages long and I could never get around to finishing it. So, I asked a young fellow to give me a name from it and I went back to the producer and said that was the only part I was prepared to play. They didn't give it to me. I have no clue to this day what the part was. For all I know it could have been a woman!"

When James Plunkett's epic novel *Strumpet City* was adapted into an RTE television series, Noel was secretly hurt that he hadn't been offered a role in the story of the Dublin of Jim Larkin. He had vivid memories of the effects upon his friends and neighbours of the lockouts, strikes, relief boats from Liverpool for the young children berthed at the North Wall, and the savage baton charge by the police in O'Connell Street when Larkin appeared at a balcony of the Imperial Hotel. It was a part of his life and city and nobody had thought to invite him to participate.

Towards the end of 1965, his old boss who became a close and valued friend, Louis Elliman, died at his home one morning while bending over and tying up his shoelaces. It is a peculiarity of Dubliners that the pain of bereavement is often met head-on, defiantly with a joke, the more caustic the better. Noel's comment on the death of his old friend and colleague was: "When I see how things happen to some of these clever fellas, thanks be to Jaysus I'm an eejit!" On the morning of the large funeral there was very heavy persistent rain and Cecil Sheridan, who had never forgiven "Mr Louis" for not trying harder to save the Royal, couldn't resist making one of his famous puns: "The Elliments were always against us!"

In February 1972 Noel received a letter from Wolf Mankowitz which detailed a production schedule for a reading of his play *The Samson Riddle* at the Gate on Sunday 19 March at 8pm. A postscript read: "A bound copy of *The Samson Riddle* will be sent to you by separate post within the next few days, giving you at least a week and a half to study the script before the reading." When the printed and bound script arrived, it was inscribed:

> For Noel Purcell—a head to launch a thousand epics—with the love of Wolf Mankowitz.

The reading at the Gate must have been an eventful occasion as it featured the following cast (roles in parentheses):

Alun Owen (Narrator, Zoab, a priest); Miriam Karlin (Samson's mother); Hilton Edwards (Manoah); Hugh Millais (Samson); Noel Purcell (a vintner, a scribe, a barber); Susannah York (Samson's Bride, Delilah); Christopher Casson (a scribe, a rabbi, a priest); Liam Miller (an elder, a priest); Patrick Dawson (a suitor, a noble), Dan (a warrior, a priest); Shireen Marcus (Delilah's maid); Doireann Ní Bhriain (a girl); Gerard McSorley (a suitor); Edward Marcus (a suitor). Lighting was by Hilton Edwards and production assistants were Gerald Davis and Serena Newby. Stage manager was Séamus Byrne.

In 1973 Noel made his last film "with that fella with the green eyes," *The Mackintosh Man,* way out in Roundstone in the west of Ireland. Noel was eighty-three at the time of telling and couldn't recall the name of "green eyes" but he knew that he was one of the famous ones. It was, of course, Paul Newman.

On 22 December 1973, Gay Byrne built his famous RTE *Late Late Show,* now the world's longest running chat show, around Noel Purcell to celebrate his 73rd birthday. This was a very occasional type of format designed to honour outstanding citizens. His previous choice a couple of years earlier had been Mícheál Mac Liammóir. Noel was visibly moved by the honour. He held Gay Byrne in very high esteem for the manner in which he presented *The Late Late Show.* A liberal and progressively minded man himself, he admired Gay's efforts to demolish sacred cows and encourage discussion about subjects which would otherwise have remained taboo in Irish society—a policy which demanded courage and in time created more open mindedness in an insular society. Eileen noticed that when the *Late Late* went off the television screens for the annual summer break, Noel noticeably suffered from withdrawal symptoms.

"I had agreed to go on the show for the usual bit of chat," said Noel, "but I didn't realise how hush-hush it was until I was introduced by Gay and when I walked on to take my seat beside him I realised that the studio was full of all my old friends and relatives. Gay had turned the show into his own kind of version of *This Is Your Life* like Éamonn's show in 1958. All my old pals were there: Eddie Byrne; Jack Cruise; Cecil Sheridan, who sang one of his latest parodies; Hector Grey; Louis Copeland; Pauline Forbes; Seán Mooney, who sang "Friend o' Mine"; Philip Green; Leo Maguire; Lorcan Bourke; Pat Taaffe; Joe Kearns; Marie Keane; and of course, Eileen and the boys." In a television link-up with the BBC, Noel received greetings from Jack Doyle, Joe Lynch, John Gregson and Bob Monkhouse in London. One of the guests that night was Peggy Dell. Many people really thought she had died until they saw and heard her play the piano just as expertly as ever on the show that night. It opened up an entirely new career for her; Adrian Cronin offered her her own television programme called *Peg o' My Heart* which ran for several series. She made two albums, and another record company re-released all her old numbers with the Jack Hylton Orchestra.

The reminiscences both funny and nostalgic and the undisguised sincerity in the compliments to Noel made it a memorable occasion and Noel obviously enjoyed it. Gay presented Noel with a Tyrone Crystal iceberg which incorporated a carving in the crystal of Noel's head and shoulders. There was a big birthday cake which was wheeled on at the end and Noel was fearful that the number of candles might burn the studio down.

Gay Byrne reported on the following week's show that the *Late Late* tribute to Noel got a tremendous reaction from all over the land. People were very fond of him and they revered him as a last remaining link with the old world of vaudeville and variety. Noel's contribution to the night was a piece by Philip Green which he had just lately recorded:

But Now I Know

When I was young and very sure
For ev'ry ill I had a cure.
I said, "I know
I know! I know! I know!"

When I was older, more mature
And not so very very sure
I said "I know;
At least I think I know."

But now I know
But now I really know
Of only one thing I am truly very sure:
That is, I wish I knew; I wish I knew.

When I was young love was my right,
A passing cloud, a pleasant night
Love was my right
And love was my delight.

Then with the passing of the years
Love brought me happiness and tears
Love was a pleasure,
A priceless treasure.

But now I know
But now I really know
Of only one thing I am truly very sure
Love is a gift; love is a gift.

Now in the September of my life,
Now I can remember all my life,
All the joys and sorrows of my life,
All the fine tomorrows of my life.

When I was young, I made my memories,
A thousand memories to live with evermore.
Then later on I had my memories.
I lived my memories a thousand times or more.

But now I know
But now I really know,
While I have hope and
Something worth hoping for.

A Biography

One little hope is worth
A thousand memories
And this I know
And this I know.

In the following year, Noel, as was his habit, sang with the Garda band and choir for an audience of old folk at a concert in County Kildare. "It was a hot day in June and I seemed to be the only one who wasn't undressed for the weather," recalled Noel. "I was overcome by the heat and I felt so weak that a kind friend brought me a chair. Then somebody brought me two tumblers—one with water, the other with whiskey. And by God I must have been ill—I drank the water."

Had Eileen been present she'd have recognised that Noel had merely succumbed to one of his occasional fainting fits but his Garda friends feared that he might have had a heart attack and arranged to take him by car immediately from Kill to Elm Park Hospital. Unfortunately the speeding car broke down and while Noel's friends worked feverishly to repair it, Noel flagged down another car and enquired of the driver if he would take him to a hospital. "I'm having a heart attack," said Noel apologetically. After exhaustive tests in Elm Park it was discovered that there was absolutely nothing wrong with him but he delighted in sending postcards to friends like Joe Kearns signed, "From the Knackers!"

CHAPTER FIFTEEN

In the late seventies William Rocke reported in one of the Dublin papers:

> Noel Purcell is back on record, almost twenty-five years after he cut his famous disc "The Dublin Saunter" on the old Glenside label, with which he topped the Irish hit parade in the early fifties. Noel's latest disc, this time on the Dolphin label, is "Brendan Behan," a tribute to a fellow Dubliner who, like Noel, became famous outside Ireland.

The tribute was written by another Dubliner, top songwriter Pete St John, who said, "Noel heard the lyric at a party and said to me 'I'd like to put that on record. It's exactly the way I remember the Quare Fella!'"

"I knew Brendan well," said Noel. "I first met him on a picnic in the Dublin mountains when we discovered we had a lot in common. Later we used to meet in the theatres in Dublin and when both of our careers took off we'd bump into each other in places like Paris, London, Berlin and New York." No matter where Brendan met Noel, he would always insist that the latter sing his famous "Dublin Saunter," the song written for him in 1954 by Leo Maguire, another Dublin Liberties boy who became a singer, broadcaster and composer. His popular "Glenside" sponsored programme was the longest running of any on Radio Éireann and he became known by the catch phrase, "If you feel like singing, do sing an Irish song." Leo said on one occasion that "Dublin Saunter" was one of several pieces written for Noel to perform during the first Tóstal in 1953. There was also "Pretty Polly," a piece about the old Dublin cabbie and his horse which actually reduced the soft-hearted Noel to tears the first time he tried it out.

Pete St John's lyrics about Behan refer to Russell Street, where he was born, and McDaid's bar in Harry Street, where he practically lived. It ends: "'Twas the fickle jar eclipsed his star, and fools will ask you why..." Amongst Noel's papers a small undated greeting card was discovered from Sacred Heart Residence, Sybil Hill, Dublin 5, which reads:

A Chara,

Many thanks for your lovely words on radio about my poor Brendan, only you made me cry. May God bless you.

Your sincere friend,
Kathleen Behan

It is an extraordinary thing that is unlikely that Noel ever received a penny for his recording of the "Dublin Saunter." This was definitely not due to a practice prevalent today amongst music managers known as "the rip-off." The facts were that Noel and Martin Walton, the publisher and producer of the record, were close and intimate old friends. Noel was by nature a very generous man and he told Walton in the presence of their mutual friend Séamus de Búrca, that if the subject of money was raised he would feel insulted. The result was that when Martin Walton received the first big royalty cheque from the Performing Rights Society for well over £1000 he gave the entire amount to Leo Maguire.

In 1976 the new Dublin impresario with innovative ideas was Noel Pearson and he and David Gordon devised a show for the Gaiety called *You Ain't Heard Nuthin' Yet!*—a salute to the American musical theatre from 1910 to 1950 as recalled by an old stage door keeper. This role was played by the seventy-five year old Noel Purcell, returning to the stage after an absence of twenty years.

The musical numbers ranged from "Alexander's Rag-Time Band" to "My Boy Bill" from *Carousel*. Gus Smith wrote in the *Sunday Independent*:

> It would be easy to dismiss the Gaiety show *You Ain't Heard Nuthin' Yet!* as nothing but sheer nostalgia. Of course this would be unjust, for the show itself is a glorious tribute to American music from 1910 to 1950. Besides being slick, colourful and sparkling, it has in Tony Kenny a gifted vocalist and showman. Those amazing troubadours Noel Purcell and Cecil Sheridan move about the stage as if they were starting their careers all over again. Both are simply captivating. I recommend this show for two reasons: the all-round entertainment—and for the performances of Tony Kenny, Noel Purcell and Cecil Sheridan...

Desmond MacAvock noted in the *Evening Press*:

> Noel Pearson has called on and combined as seemingly only he knows how to, the considerable talents of a large number of artists ranging from the venerable Noel Purcell and Cecil Sheridan to the personable Tony Kenny. Cecil Sheridan in his own spot combined with wit, ease and immensely practised skill a whole series of reminders of stars of the past....

This was a truly fitting final notice for Cecil Sheridan; the show was his swan-song and he never appeared again. In the final analysis Cecil was wrong on the night that he stood in the foyer of the Theatre Royal with Louis Elliman observing a group of newspaper critics arriving to review the show when he turned to "Mr Louis" and commented, "Here comes the pilgrimage to Knock!"

When the show transferred to Cork, the *Cork Examiner* reported:

> It is the musical show of the decade. It stars Tony Kenny who is at his very best and will certainly endear himself to the hearts of the older generation. He is superb in his tribute to Al Jolson* with songs like "Mammy," "Babyface," "April Showers," and "Rosie." Cecil Sheridan and Noel Purcell come together to render "Try to Remember" and have the audience near to tears with this nostalgic song. However, they very quickly dry all eyes with a clever and hilarious piece, "Brush Up Your Shakespeare."

Noel sang "September Song" which he repeated later on several occasions on radio and television. His dialogue for the show was written by himself and Alan Simpson. The production was staged and choreographed by Domy Reiter-Soffer. Noel and Tony Kenny became firm friends and Noel took a keen interest in the younger performer, seeing perhaps a reflection of himself fifty years earlier. One evening Noel called Tony aside and pointing to some stage props he said: "You know, these things were meant to be used not thrown into some corner to be forgotten and gather dust," and he presented Tony with his top-hat, silver-topped cane and white evening gloves. So, whenever Tony appears nowadays using these props, audiences should remember that Noel isn't too far away.

In December of that year, Noel starred in Pearson's musical fantasia *Cinderella's Christmas Dream* in Goff's, Kill, County Kildare, a venue that was used increasingly for such productions. He was

---

* Jolson must surely have inspired the title of the show since it was his catchphrase.

making regular radio broadcasts on religious themes and he was to be seen occasionally on television. He was Peggy Dell's guest star in one edition of her show *Peg o' My Heart* and together they performed an old act, familiar to both of them from the old Royal days—"Thank you Ma'm Says Dan." In January 1978 he did a series of six programmes of talks with Pádraig Ó Raghallaigh on Radio and in the same year Noel Pearson cast him as Jacob in his remarkable production of *Joseph and the Amazing Technicolor Dreamcoat* with Tony Kenny as a splendid Joseph at the Gaiety Theatre and later at Goff's. Noel was described by the press as "rejuvenated, involved and looking like a bearded God." Desmond Rushe of the *Irish Independent* thought that "Noel Purcell's venerable Jacob could have stepped straight out of a Renaissance painting..." It was to be Noel's last stage show and it seemed appropriate that it should have included "a delightfully tuneful Synge Street boy soprano chorus." Tim Rice, the librettist, was persuaded to write in a special additional verse in one of Noel's songs—significantly it had something to do with horse racing!

In 1980 Noel presented a special Easter Sunday programme on RTE Radio 1 called *Reared on Tales and Stories* produced and compiled by Brian Reynolds. It was an impressionistic journey in time and space through a capital city (Dublin) as seen by a variety of poets, authors and musicians, in a selection of new material specially commissioned for the programme.

In 1981 Noel appeared to be suffering from a prolonged bout of laryngitis so he consulted his friend Dr Joe Millar who sent him to see a specialist in Fitzwilliam Square, and he was sent for tests to St Luke's Hospital, Rathgar, where it was discovered that he had cancer of the larynx. He attended the hospital for treatment as an out-patient, but as a result of the bitterly cold weather he got pneumonia and was hospitalised in the Adelaide Hospital. On his 81st birthday in December, his family had to restrict the number of visitors as he was still having to use oxygen to assist his breathing and they thought that he would be unable to cope

with the number of well-wishers anxious about his health. In fact
he had had a relapse earlier in the week and would be unable to
go home for Christmas. Nevertheless, many old show business
friends talked an extremely worried Eileen into letting them in
for a quick visit just to wish him a "Happy Birthday" and someone
even managed to wheel in a trolley of champagne. Noel informed
his visitors—among them were Philip Green, the composer, Gay
Byrne and Hal Roach— "I don't know why you've all come because
I have no intention of going anywhere—yet!"

Another visitor was Joe Lynch, a long time admirer of Noel,
who when he was making the long-running BBC series *Never
Mind the Quality, Feel the Width* admitted that he had based his
character of an Irish tailor on the personality of the young Noel
Purcell. Eileen and her sons, Mike, Glynn and Victor, with two
grand-daughters, Zara and Tiffany, were there also, but when the
President of Ireland, Dr Patrick Hillery, walked in to convey his
good wishes, Noel raised his dark eyebrows in astonishment and
he was as close to being completely speechless as it was possible
for him to be. Apparently Joe Kearns had that morning rung Áras
an Uachtaráin to ask if President Hillery would send Noel a get-
well telegram. The President's secretary asked him to hold on and
returned to say that not only would the President send a telegram
but he'd pay Noel a visit as well.

At the hospital all the nurses were lined up outside Noel's
room awaiting the President and when he arrived he greeted
everyone and then marched straight into Noel's room and
presented him with a gift of a bottle of whiskey. It did Noel the
power of good.

"I was only in medical school when I met you first," recalled
Dr Hillery.

"Ah, you were only a young fella then," said Noel sadly.

"I remember seeing you with Eddie Byrne and Joe Locke," said
the distinguished visitor.

"Ah, the good old days in the Royal," said Noel, eyes sparkling.

"And the Royalettes," mused the President.

Despite protests that his voice was gone, Noel was persuaded to sing into a tape recorder for RTE the song inseparably connected with him in the public mind, "The Dublin Saunter."

After his recovery in the Adelaide, he was transferred to St Luke's as an in-patient. There treatment on his larnyx was resumed. He never complained and didn't appear to be in severe pain. When he was discharged his voice was weaker and on his few subsequent public appearances he was obviously very hoarse and the emotion-filled occasions were almost too much for him.

We did say that Noel had made his last stage appearance in *Joseph and the Amazing Technicolor Dreamcoat*, but it is a fact that opera lovers seated in the Gaiety theatre on the evening of Tuesday 13 April 1982 fancied that the Cardinal in Act One of *Tosca* looked remarkably like Noel Purcell. And they were right. It wasn't a singing role, of course, but he bestowed silent benedictions all round and no one except those on the stage with him realised that he was muttering the odds like a tic-tac man at the races.

Noel's return to the stage, however brief, was as much a surprise to him as it was to the audience. He had gone backstage to wish his great friend, Michele Molese, who was singing the role of Mario Cavardossi, good luck before the first night performance when he found himself being made-up and costumed. Noel said happily, "It was great being back on the old Gaiety stage again, but they got me off just in time. I wouldn't have lasted another second, the bloody legs were going from under me."

Naturally this wasn't the first time that Signor Purcell had appeared in opera. Twenty years previously he had just come back from Hollywood and he wanted to get in to hear di Stefano sing in *Tosca* at any price, but there wasn't a seat or standing room to be had. Colonel Bill O'Kelly, one of the leading lights of the Dublin Grand Opera Society, came up with an ingenious solution that appealed to Noel. He suggested that he could go on as the Cardinal and stand next to di Stefano on stage, which he did. Michele Molese who was a personal friend of Noel and Eileen knew about this and said, "There is an Italian saying: 'There's never two without three.' Now with another production of *Tosca*, Noel has to be in it." Both di Stefano and Molese were regular visitors to Sandymount. Noel didn't appear in opera again but he hadn't quite made his last appearance on the stage of the Gaiety.

CHAPTER SIXTEEN

During his long lifetime "me ould brown" or "the long fellow" had been the recipient of honours, great and small. On one occasion he was crowned "King of Dalkey Island." The island is a lump of rock off the coast at Dalkey, County Dublin, which lays claim to a time-misted right to elect its own monarch and to celebrate the occasion with an annual crowning ceremony with civic dignitaries in attendance. In other words another excuse for an Irish hooley.

Although he was known jokingly in Hollywood as the "Dublin Rabbi" thanks to Danny Kaye, the Jewish community had taken him to its heart just as it had in Dublin. His reputation had spread across the US and on the occasion of the second annual banquet of the Loyal League of Yiddish Sons of Erin, held on St Patrick's Day 1963 at Moskowitz and Lupowitz of 40 Second Avenue (Corner 2nd Street), New York City, Mr Noel Purcell was elected an honorary member. The kosher menu contained such genuine attempts at Irishness as Green Maraschino cherries, Dill Pickles Killarney, Green Matzah Balls à la Dublin, Irish Potato, Green Vegetables and Sherbet à la River Shannon. In common brotherhood the toasts were to "Erin go Bragh" and "Shalom." Old Maurice Elliman, the founder of the Elliman dynasty, would have been impressed.

On 7 December 1971 in honour of his long and devoted service to the Irish theatre, Noel was elected to life membership of the Irish Actors' Equity Association and so joined such distinguished former recipients as May Craig, Lady Christine Longford, Eileen Crowe, Harry Brogan, Maureen Potter, Siobhán McKenna, Jimmy O'Dea and Isobel Couser.

On 1 January 1971, Brother PJ Noel Purcell (6/238) was made an honorary life member of the Order of the Knights of St Columbanus in recognition of his continuous faithful service during twenty-five years years and upwards.

In June 1984 the council of Actors' Equity (United Kingdom) awarded honorary life membership to Noel Purcell for his outstanding service to the acting profession and their Unions in Britain and Ireland.

But the ultimate and supreme honour was yet to come.

On 22 June 1984 at a special meeting of Dublin City Council the Lord Mayor, Michael Keating, moved the motion to confer the civic honour of the Freedom of the City on Noel Purcell and Maureen Potter. The Lord Mayor recalled the decades of entertainment which they had given: they were two very distinguished people who represented the spirit of Dublin. He recalled, also, the humour created by Jimmy O'Dea and Maureen Potter and said that Noel Purcell represented the humour, grandeur and dignity of the city. When Noel was informed that the city council had decided to make him a freeman on Thursday 28 June 1984, he said that he was really flabbergasted because he was not worthy of such a great honour. He added, "But I'm delighted. In our business we are still rogues and vagabonds and yet we are chosen these days for an honour like this. It's very nice and I hope that I will become worthy of the freedom of my native city."

From the end of the twelfth century there were many categories of admission to the freedom of the city, with conditions usually involving religious denomination, exclusion of the Irish nation, money, birth, marriage etc. In 1876 a new category of honorary freedom of the city was introduced and this is still in force today. Maureen Potter was only the second freewoman ever; the other was Lady Sandhurst who was honoured in 1889. But Noel joined a list of distinguished men like General Ulysses F Grant, Charles Stewart Parnell, John F Kennedy, Éamon de Valera, John A Costello, John Count McCormack, George Bernard Shaw, Hilton Edwards, Mícheál Mac Liammóir and the most recent of the fifty-three recipients, Pope John Paul II who received the honour in 1979. On the evening of the great event many people gathered outside the Mansion House in a light drizzle to applaud Noel and Maureen. The Gardaí were kept busy organising the crowd and keeping the traffic moving and the red carpet was unrolled an hour before the arrival of the invited guests, who included old colleagues Harry Bailey, Pauline Forbes, Danny Cummins, Ursula Doyle, Vernon Hayden, Seán Mooney, Séamus de Búrca and the celebrated Connie Ryan (who long long ago had taught Noel to dance in *Irish Smiles*). After a reception in the Oak Room at seven o'clock they took their seats in the Round Room. The Lord Mayor and the city councillors, all in their robes of office complete with tricorne hats, were seated on the stage. The city manager, Frank Feely, was present, the only official without headwear, the absence of which, as was once explained humorously by Myles na Gopaleen, being "to prevent the city manager from talking through his hat."

The band of the Curragh Command played as the Dublin Corporation choir sang "The Dublin Saunter" and the huge mayoral mace and sword, which date from 1403, were borne in by two uniformed ushers. Noel and Maureen followed directly behind with Noel seated in a wheelchair waving his great arms conductor-style. He was assisted on to the stage to his place at a richly covered table. Two clips from *The Rising of the Moon* in which both Noel and Maureen appeared (although in different sections), were shown.

When the Lord Mayor rose to speak he said that the city council was conferring the civic honour of the freedom of the

city on these two wonderful people because of the great work
they had done in uplifting the human spirit over so many decades
and in so many different parts of the world. They had brought
much happiness to many lives. Dublin was honoured to honour
them and they would be esteemed for generations to come. He
said that "love" was an inadequate word to express their feelings
for the pair; if any town had darlings, Noel and Maureen were the
darlings of our capital city. Their achievement was profound. It
was not remembered in stone or glass or concrete, but it was
more deeply etched in the hearts and minds of the thousands
who have enjoyed their performances down the years.

The formal resolution making the two "freemen" was read out
by Frank Feely, and Noel signed the register first with obvious
pride directly under the signature of Pope John Paul II. Maureen
signed her name and added the name O'Leary (her marriage name)
beside it in parentheses. The band played "There's No Business
Like Show Business" as the guests gave a standing ovation. For a
brief moment, as chins and lower lips quivered, and there was a
noticeable quick blinking of eyelids, it looked as if everyone was
going to cry. In fact, the occasion can only be described as full
of memories for so many people who had spent happy hours in
the now demolished Queen's and Capitol Theatres and above all
in the wonderland of the Theatre Royal. Memories of Dublin in
the rare oul' times were still fresh in their minds. Noel replied in
a verse written for him by his old friend Leo Maguire:

Friends! Romans! Countrymen [*whispered*] That's not my proper
cue!
It's my own darlin' Dubliners that I am talking to,
Friends old and new, all tried and true, who've honoured me
today
It makes me feel so humble: but this I'd like to say:
If some fairy waved her wand and offered me the earth,
I'd rather be a Freeman in the city of my birth.

My wanderings have taken me to countries strange and far,
From Iceland to the Tropic Isles, but lovely as they are
I didn't weep when leaving them, my heart was never there:
'Twas calling me to hurry home to Dublin City fair,
To York Street, Cork Street, Meath Street and the Coombe,
I know them all, I've walked them all when I was in full bloom,
I love the little houses where the decent people live,
The open-handed people who haven't much to give.
God bless them all! God bless us too, and send us all his peace!
May kindliness and friendship in old Dublin never cease.
Dear Old Dublin! Lovely Dublin! May you ever lovelier grow,
As long as leaves grow on the trees and Liffey waters flow.

My Lord Mayor, Ladies and Gentlemen, once more, from the depths of my heart I say, "God bless us all and send us his peace!"

Afterwards at a reception in the Supper Room Noel said:

It's a great honour. I never expected it. You really associate honours like this with physicists, doctors and architects. Here am I an ex-carpenter, getting it. I am not worthy of it but I'm deeply, deeply honoured; but I knew an old comic one time who had a good line—he used to say, "There's no fun in the cemetery. Just give me the flowers now!" That's how I feel.

The reception in the Supper Room consisted of wine and savouries but at 9.15 there was music and dancing with a bar available. There can be no doubt that at that stage someone got Noel a real jar—a ball of malt!

The honour bestowed upon him was a very popular one with all sections of society as the following letter illustrates:

Office of the Taoiseach
28 June 1984.

Dear Noel,

Joan and I are very pleased that you are to receive the Freedom of
the City of Dublin. Your contribution to the world of entertainment
over such a long and distinguished career has been outstanding. The
sheer variety and excellence of your performances on stage and on
screen have brought great pleasure to many generations and enhanced
the reputation of this country. It is fitting that Dublin Corporation
should acknowledge your achievements in this fashion. We are sorry
that we will not be able to be present on this historic occasion but we
would like to extend our warmest congratulations and best wishes.

With kind regards
Yours warmly,
Garret FitzGerald
Taoiseach

Noel wrote to the Lord Mayor:

4 Wilfield Road
Ballsbridge
Dublin 4
1st July 1984

The Right Honourable Michael Keating TD
Lord Mayor of Dublin
Mansion House
Dublin 2

My Lord Mayor,

You, your fellow Corporators and your Staff have done me an
honour far greater than I could have anticipated.

There have been many highlights, many outstanding occasions in
my long and very happy career; but the conferring of the Honorary
Freedom of my Native City on me was the crowning glory.

NOEL PURCELL

It is something I shall always cherish.

I want to thank everyone connected with the conferring for the wonderful organisation that made the whole function so gloriously memorable.

In deepest gratitude,

Your devoted Citizen,
Noel Purcell

CHAPTER SEVENTEEN

Eileen was surprised and relieved that Noel, after such a full and eventful life, accepted retirement with equanimity. He accepted his long life with gratitude. "That's eighty-three years of my life," he told her on his birthday, "a dacent ol' life among dacent people, I'd say." He spent his days in his graceful home, surrounded by his piano and individual pieces of furniture that had been chosen over the years with an aesthetically discerning eye. Noel had inherited an appreciation of antiques from his mother but it was Eileen who was the connoisseur behind the collection of finely-carved furniture and impressive silver ornaments and plate. One exceptionally fine sideboard was thought to be the work of the master craftsman, James Hicks. Some particularly fine and rare photographs, scrolls and drawings illustrating highlights in his career decorated the walls but one that he had treasured most was missing. This was a drawing that Sophia Loren had done of him while they drank tea from thick mugs during a break in the filming of *The Millionairess* around 1960. "She was a beautiful unassuming lady," said Noel, "who didn't give a thought to drinking from a mug suitable only for a navvy," and she was genuinely embarrassed when Noel asked her to sign her excellent drawing of him. Unfortunately it was stolen from his dressing room. In a corner by the window on a tall column stood an impressive bust of his leonine head. This bust had an extraordinary history. Noel sat for a sculptor called Mrs Smyth of Greystones when he was living in Sydney Parade. The lady eventually delivered it personally one morning. She gave little information about herself, refused to accept any payment and has never been seen since.

A complete dinner service, Harry O'Donovan's wedding present to them, had survived intact for almost fifty years and was displayed in a tall corner unit. Noel didn't, despite popular belief, use a wheelchair at home, but as his hands could not grasp a walking stick, he achieved mobility by holding on to the furniture—or his friends. Séamus de Búrca relates that he visited Noel one morning, when he was alone in the house, to discuss his historically valuable book *The Queen's Royal Theatre*, and when Noel met him at the door he said, "D'ye mind if I put me arm around you and lean on you, son?"

Eileen obtained books for him from the RDS library; he loved books about movies and they laughed together over a particular book he'd read three times, *How to Make a Jewish Movie*. He watched a lot of sport on television, particularly horse-racing and snooker, but some of the movies disgusted him. He told Clare Boylan, "The only thing that makes me sad when I look back is the death of the music-hall. In the old days you were expected to do everything and you did it. Nowadays it sometimes seems that the only place an actor has to have any talent is in bed. I can't get used to these new films where personal matters are turned into public entertainment."

Many old friends were regular visitors: Joe Kearns kept him up-to-date with the news from theatreland; Larry Flood, another old friend, chatted about times past and Joe Dillon the photographer from Tuam spent a lot of time with Noel. One result was his impressive photograph of Noel in his declining years which hangs in the Gaiety and reflects the very essence of the man—his openness, humility, great wisdom and understanding in the expression in the hazel eyes and dignity, great dignity. Strangely, the study does not capture any humour, but then that would have been superfluous—the subject of the study is obvious. Seeing it brings back a flood of memories of half-forgotten comedy routines—Nedser and Nuala, Conn of the Hundred Fights and Doody the doleful jockey, literally doubled in two as a result of his pessimism singing "I've Gotter Motter" from *The Arcadians*, all delivered in a distinctive, never-to-be-forgotten voice.

He often reminded his visitors about the old Theatre Royal days, when admission to the complete programme cost one shilling. "But that was Dublin in those days," he recalled. "Everything was cheap. If you put a shilling in a machine you'd get twenty cigarettes and a halfpenny change. But don't let anyone cod you. Dublin was a lovable city, and still is a wonderful city despite the fact that much of its buildings are gone, but to put it in a nutshell these are the good old days. We never had it so good.* That Shangri-La we used to call Dublin in the 'balmy' days...well they were rough times."

But he had some reservations about modern living. He said, "I'm an old-fashioned man. I believe that credit is the curse of the world today. A man should be able to pay his way all along—live decently and be buried decently, and I consider birth to be more alarming than death." He often told his sons that his own number was in the frame but he had already had his own awesome premonition of death which he could never explain or understand. The incident concerns Noel's role of King David in *Solomon and Sheba* which was shot in Spain and starred Tyrone Power and Gina Lollobrigida (more beautiful off the screen than she was on it and a lovely person according to Noel). One morning Noel was filming his final scene in the film in which he is supposed to be dying and he summons his son, played by Tyrone Power, to his death-bed. When Power came into shot Noel could not control

---

* Noel was speaking during the early 1980s.

the tears rolling down his cheeks; Power kissed him on the forehead and there was a little dialogue in the two-minute sequence. Soon Noel and Power, who had been affectionate friends for many years, were weeping uncontrollably, quite without reason and in disproportion to the requirements of the scene. Finally, the director, King Vidor, called, "Cut, that's it, print that one." They had achieved in a few minutes what could normally be expected to take a day to obtain.

Noel came back to Dublin for a fortnight and then went to Hong Kong to film with Orson Welles. One day when he had been there a couple of weeks he was going up in the lift at his hotel after shooting some night scenes in Hong Kong when the liftman said to him, "I suppose you heard that your son is dead?" The badly-shaken Noel eventually learned that Tyrone Power had just died from a heart attack while filming a sword fight with George Sanders. Noel couldn't sleep that night, his head was full of his final scene with Power and the unexplained tears. "It was as if I knew," said Noel quietly, "that this man would die within a month."

He told Joe Kearns, "Hard work is the secret of a long life— it was also my hobby. I smoked twenty cigarettes a day, enjoyed the odd jar, and never bothered with exercise. Life is never predictable. I didn't get married until I was forty one. When I was forty six I became a film star. I'm luckier than most men in that I've done almost everything I ever wanted." Almost everything. He did have his disappointments. The greatest was when John Huston played the role of Noah in *The Greatest Story Ever Told* instead of thinking of Noel for the part, and he was also sad when Otto Preminger had not thought to invite him to appear in *Exodus*. He confided, "For those two films I would have worked for nothing." But his biggest unfulfilled wish was to sing Philip Green's song "Suffer Little Children to Come unto Me" surrounded by children.

He delighted in recounting stories of his encounters with some of the great classical artists whom Louis Elliman attracted to the Theatre Royal for Saturday afternoon celebrity concerts. On one particular Saturday morning after the resident company had finished their dress rehearsal for the following week's show, Noel sat in the stalls with his young son Glynn while the concert piano was wheeled on stage so that the great pianist José Iturbi could try it out. Iturbi, with a pipe stuck in the side of his mouth much in the style of Bing Crosby, played chords and short passages. When he finally arose from the piano-stool, Noel stood up in the stalls and said, "Maestro, while you're warming up the piano would you ever do me the favour of playing a favourite piece of mine—Debussy's 'Claire de Lune'?" Iturbi stopped in his tracks, scratched his head and frowning said, "I'm sorry, but I'm afraid I don't know it!" And it was true. He joined Noel in the stalls and was introduced to Glynn, which sparked off an amusing conversation about his own grandchildren at home in America.

On another occasion, in Tahiti, Noel and Eddie Byrne decided to take a car drive around the island, "a beautiful place," according to Noel, "if you're a Tahitian!" After driving ten miles into the interior they decided to have some refreshments in a wayside hotel. They were sitting having their drinks when Noel on glancing around the lounge spotted the diminutive figure of Lily Pons. He couldn't believe it, but he approached her and introduced himself and Eddie, and explained that they were filming *Mutiny on the Bounty*. Madame Pons sipped her coffee and displayed great interest and explained that she herself was on holiday. Just as Noel was about to take his leave he asked, "Madam, do you ever sing at all now?"

"Only for my own amusement," said the great diva sadly.

"Talking about Tahiti," Noel would say, warming to his subject, "did I ever tell you about Brando? A grand fella and, let nobody cod you, a great actor; and he wasn't a bad warbler himself in *Guys and Dolls*. Well, one night Eddie and myself and Dickie Harris were havin' a bit of a singsong when in walks Brando and he was so delighted with it that I declare to me God we had to sing at least a half a dozen times for him that ould come-all-ye 'Get up outa that you impudent brat and let Mr Maguire sit down.'"

Another man who impressed Noel was Ernest Gold who wrote the music for *Exodus* and whom he met at Harpo Marx's house in Hollywood. It was only in private conversation with Noel that one ever heard these names being mentioned (he mentioned them in letters to Eileen, of course) but they never found their way into interviews with the press. To him being a name-dropper was a cardinal sin. His favourite LPs in his record rack were those by Maria Callas—he probably met her too but he'd never tell you!

In October 1984 the Gaiety Theatre was re-opened after a £750,000 facelift. Tickets were £25 a head which included a champagne reception. The President Dr Hillery and his wife Maeve attended the show which was called *Night of a Hundred Stars* and was memorable for, among other items, Peter O'Toole's reading of Swift's "A Modest Proposal" in its entirety. Next day the *Irish Independent* report ended:

> There were stars aplenty but none shone so brightly as the Old Lady of South King Street. Noel Purcell, making a triumphant entrance in his wheelchair at the finale, propelled on stage by Gay Byrne, was the second big star. "Dublin Can be Heaven" sang Frank Paterson and the chorus of the Rathmines and Rathgar Musical Society. The audience rose spontaneously in tribute and the veteran actor...wiped a tear from his eye.

The *Sunday Independent* reported:

> "No report of this sparkling nostalgic evening would be complete without mention of the final highlight that brought the house down—the surprise entrance of the one and only Noel Purcell. Now sadly confined to a wheelchair, the grand old man of the

Dublin theatre had tears in his eyes as he conducted a few bars
of "Grafton Street's a Wonderland"—and the audience roared.

Ten days before his eighty-fourth birthday, on 13 December 1984,
the Variety Club of Ireland Tent 41 organised a tribute to Noel at
the Burlington Hotel. There were 500 guests and all were personal
friends. The cabaret was called *Pete St John's "Tribute to Noel Purcell"*
and included another famous "Dubliner" Ronnie Drew. Noel's
response was to make a large, exaggerated sign of the cross saying
"Share that out amongst you!" And still the courageous old man
wasn't finished. In January 1985, a month before his death, he
made his last professional appearance in an episode of the
television series *The Irish RM* adapted from the stories of Somerville
and Ross. He was seated throughout the episode but that did not
deter him from giving a noteworthy performance—something
that would have met with the approval of the tradesman in him.
During the Variety Club of Ireland's tribute, Noel was asked to
nominate the charity to which he would prefer them to donate
a new ambulance. Without hesitation he said the Cerebral Palsy
workers in Sandymount and the ambulance bearing his name
and that of the Variety Club was presented to them.

In 1974 Noel had been the recipient of the VATS (Variety
Artists' Trust Society) annual award. In a programme tribute Cecil
Sheridan had written:

Today the VATS pay tribute to an artist who has graced the
theatrical profession over more than fifty years and in that time
has gained the admiration not alone of his fellow artists but
audiences of millions through the media of stage, radio, films
and television.

His undoubted success has not changed this man in so far as
he is today the same natural Dubliner so beloved by all who
knew him, be they humble or higher ups.

From call-boy in the Gaiety at the age of twelve until today, he has lived and loved the world of entertainment in its many spheres, and in return it has loved him.

Irish audiences will never forget his "Nedser and Nuala" sketches with Eddie Byrne in the Theatre Royal, brilliantly written by the late Dick Forbes who also penned his classical "Park Keeper" monologue which helped to lift the sad faces in the depressive war years from 1939 when Irish artists stepped in and kept the Irish theatres open, only alas to lose them when the war was over. So ladies and gentlemen, raise your glasses and the toast is: Lots of health and happiness to the ould brown son 'the long fellow'."

A résumé of Noel's life in the programme concluded:

Undoubtedly members of the audience tonight have ambitions. It would be interesting to see how many measure up to Noel's, which is "To die happy."

In February 1985, Noel and Eileen were preparing for bed one night. Eileen remained behind attending to all the chores of locking up while Noel went ahead of her. The staircase was designed with four preliminary steps, then a small landing at an angle before continuing straight up. Noel lost his grip on the short length of balustrade and fell head over heels backwards. Eileen rushed to his assistance, but he assured her that he was all right and reminded her that he knew how to fall after years of experience on the stage. He rested for a short time on the bottom step and sipped a little brandy. Next morning he was down to breakfast as usual and wondered if one of his pals would take him for a drive with the obligatory stop for a jar on the way. He hated pubs with television sets and claimed that you always had to have your own supply of cotton wool if you drank in them. When Eileen awoke on the following morning she didn't like the look of Noel: he seemed to be staring unnaturally at the ceiling and she summoned a doctor straight away. She explained the circumstances of Noel's recent fall. The doctor diagnosed pneumonia brought on by shock and asked Noel where he would prefer to be hospitalised. "Oh, the Adelaide, of course," replied Noel.

An ambulance was called and with siren screaming and lights flashing Eileen said to one of the ambulance men, "Oh my God, I've forgotten his bottle of whiskey—he's sure to want to treat his visitors."

"No problem," said the ambulance man, "there's an off-licence just down the road." So this vehicle of mercy displaying every indication of urgency stopped outside the off-licence and a bottle of restorative was secured. There was no private room available at the time but the matron promised that Noel would be transferred as soon as one was vacated; Eileen asked that he be left where he was with the two or three other patients as he liked people and company and appeared to be happy where he was. The medication produced side effects and Noel was in and out of delirium, and Eileen summoned home the members of the family who were in England, and Patrick was sent for from Australia. In the midst of her anxiety Eileen admits to some amusing moments. Noel appeared to be very upset one day and he said to Eileen, using one of his favourite expressions when he was really annoyed, "Come here," he said. "I'm fit to be tied!"

"What's wrong, Noel?"

"Do you see that man in the bed over there? They're making a picture about him and I'm not in it. They're working around me as if I wasn't here." Of course there wasn't a camera in sight.

On another occasion he appeared to be fascinated by the curtain runner around his bed and invited one of his visitors, Brian McSharry, to draw the curtains and put his hands up to examine the mechanics of the thing. "Bloody marvellous," was Noel's verdict and probably confusing the whole thing with curtains that had gone up and down and across all his life on the stage.

He was moved to another ward and seemed to have recovered sufficiently to be allowed walk up and down for exercise preparatory to going home. Mike decided that a bathroom and toilet should be constructed on the ground floor at home for Noel's convenience, and on a Saturday afternoon Eileen deferred her visit to the hospital in order to make the necessary arrangements regarding the job with a plumber. Just as Vic was telling her that his father didn't seem to be as well as he had been, the hospital rang to ask her to come to see Noel, adding that his condition had deteriorated. Very distressed, Eileen decided that it would be unwise of her to drive herself and rang Pam, Mike's wife, and asked her to drive. When they arrived, Noel was sitting up in his bed chatting animatedly with the nurses and telling them stories. Eileen looked at the ward sister, who informed her that the patient had definitely improved since she made the phone call. Eileen naturally volunteered to stay by his bedside but Noel overheard her and said, "What in the name...What would you be sitting here looking at me for. Go home, I'm OK. I'm fine." Eileen looked at the sister for guidance. "We'll ring you if there's any change," she was assured, so she went home, but couldn't sleep. An urgent call came at eight o'clock the following morning. Noel was just lying there motionless and shortly after Eileen's arrival a Carmelite father came and anointed him. Eileen put her arms around him and tried to establish contact with him. She told him that there had been a man on the telly the previous evening who had won the Irish sweep years before with the horse Nicholas Silver. Eileen and her mother Mamie always had a few bob each way on the National and as Noel was going over to see it that year with his pals Hector Grey and Willie Tyrrell they gave him a few shillings to back Nicholas Silver as it was the only grey in the race. Noel had said it hadn't a chance, but it won.

"Nicholas Silver, Noel—do you remember him?"

He nodded and Eileen was thrilled to bits, he had heard her. Next thing he sat bolt upright in the bed and she asked him if he was thirsty. He didn't open his eyes but nodded and she was sure he thought she was going to get a half one and regretted that she hadn't got one. Vic gave him a drink of water and he lay back uneasily. Eileen thought he might be uncomfortable and, slipping her arm from around him, went to find a nurse. She left Vic holding his hand and in her absence he turned his head and ended his final scene. It was Sunday 3 March 1985. The nurses who witnessed many such deaths were in tears. Who can know what anguish Eileen experienced? Today, resigned to her loss, she feels his presence everywhere. "He had been in my life since I was eleven years of age. He was a good man, a charitable man, and above all an extraordinary man," she recalls sadly.

The remains were removed to the church of Our Lady Star of the Sea, Sandymount, at 5.15 where the Lord Mayor, Michael O'Halloran, provided a flag of the city of Dublin to drape the coffin of its freeman. The coffin was received by the Rev Michael Wall, CC. The crowd of mourners was vast and distinguished— with representatives from the spheres of politics, theatre, variety, music, horse-racing, films, Garda Síochána and the hotel world. It wasn't quite summer but it was a sunny morning—a day for a stroll in Stephen's Green as Dubliners in their hundreds turned out to bid their last farewell after the Requiem Mass at 11 am on Tuesday 5 March. The officiating priest was Fr Patrick Rice PP and Bishop Joseph Carroll presided. Noel's old friend Seán Mooney and members of the Dublin Grand Opera Society sang during the Mass. Burial was at Dean's Grange Cemetery. Chief mourners were his widow Eileen, and his sons Michael, Glynn and Victor. Patrick had had to return to Australia after visiting his father days before.

Victor summed up his father for the rest of his brothers:

He was a warm, kind-hearted father and we all loved him very dearly. He was also a most amazing man. There are countless extraordinary things we will remember him for. For instance, on the morning of the Mahommed Ali–Sonny Liston fight, the house was packed with opera people at 4am waiting to see the fight on

telly and in the meantime they were singing their hearts out—
you could hear the glassware tingling on the sideboard. Only
Dad could have stage-managed a scene like that.

And what remains? Noel's work in films can still be seen and
appraised. His gramophone recordings are a testament to a great
monologuist with a distinctive captivating voice. The range and
variety of his stage appearances were astonishing, but who can
really describe a stage performance? Those who never saw him
must rely upon the acclaim he received from contemporary critics
of the time and from audiences in their thousands who paid hard
cash to see him week after week for years in the Royal and later
at the Gaiety. His greatest assets were his talents as an entertainer
(apart from his undoubted power as a straight actor) and a
magnetic sympathetic personality that held the secret of making
ordinary things appear extraordinary, bright and colourful and
above all gently humorous.

Noel Purcell, the private man, was as he has been described in
these pages, but no doubt he would be remembered in a different
light by those who met him only when he was worried or testy
or irritated or impatient—human traits which are only a very
occasional measure of the man. Readers of biographies sometimes
complain that the author never gets under the subject's skin. We
cannot know absolutely everything about anyone: even those
living close to them for years do not know their most private
thoughts or opinions. To expect such minute anatomising is as
nonsensical as expecting that one should get under the skin of an
onion. Noel Purcell was an exclusive one-off personality,
entertainer and actor. There was nothing else; the mask was the
face.

Noel, as was customary, would like the last word himself, but
we shall have to make the selection for him. He seemed to sum
himself up in the following extraordinarily reasonable way in an
interview with Clare Boylan in 1976:

If you see anyone that's been in the business as long as I have you can't help being reminded of the old music hall song that went like this:

> "Put yourself in Gilligan's place and see what you would do:
> You're on a plank that's made for one, it will not carry two,
> So Gilligan chucked the Chinaman into the raging main,
> And if you'd a been in Gilligan's place, you'd 'a' done the bloody same."

Meaning?

"Meaning," said Noel with a decided twinkle, "don't take me too seriously. And don't make me out to be an awful swell-headed oul-fella. Oh, and woudja put in a bit about me pal, Hector Grey. He's not only me bosom pal—he's me racing pal too."

FILMOGRAPHY

Noel claimed to have made close on one hundred films. The following are the most important. Film company dates are erratic: some record the year in which a film was made but the following are dated by the year in which the film was released.

1935 *Jimmy Boy* (GB) (Baxter & Barter) Director: John Baxter
Jimmy O'Dea, Guy Middleton, Enid Stamp Taylor

1938 *Blarney* (Ireland) aka *Ireland's Border Line* (O'D Productions) Director: Harry O'Donovan
Jimmy O'Dea, Myrette Morven, Hazel Hughes

1946 *Odd Man Out* (GB) (Two Cities) Director: Carol Reed
James Mason, Robert Newton, FJ McCormick, Kathleen Ryan

1947 *Captain Boycott* (GB) (Individual) Director: Frank Launder
Stewart Granger, Alastair Sim, Robert Donat

1948 *Saints and Sinners* (GB) (London Films) Director: Leslie Arliss
Kieron Moore, Christine Norden, MJ Dolan

1949 *The Blue Lagoon* (GB) (Individual) Director: Frank Launder

Jean Simmons, Donald Houston, Cyril Cusack

1950 *Talk of a Million* (GB) Director: John Paddy Carstairs
Jack Hawkins, Barbara Mullen

1951 *Appointment with Venus* (GB) (Betty E Box) Director: Ralph
Thomas
David Niven, Glynis Johns, George Coulouris

Encore—Three stories by Somerset Maugham (GB) (Two
Cities) "Winter Cruise" Director: Anthony Pelissier
Kay Walsh, Ronald Squire, Ronald Culver, John Laurie

No Resting Place (GB) (Colin Lesslie) Director: Paul Rotha
Michael Gough, Jack McGowran, Eithne Dunne

1952 *The Crimson Pirate* (USA) (Warner: Harold Hecht) Dir 'or:
Robert Siodmak
Burt Lancaster, Eva Bartok, James Hayter

Decameron Nights (GB) (MJ Frankovich) Director: Hugo
Fregonese
Louis Jourdan, Joan Fontaine, Joan Collins

Father's Doing Fine (GB) (Marble Arch) Director: Henry Cass
Heather Thatcher, Richard Attenborough

1952 *The Pickwick Papers* (GB) (George Minter) Director: Noel
Langley
James Hayter, Nigel Patrick, Donald Wolfit

1953 *Grand National Night* (GB) (George Minter) Director: Bob
McNaught
Nigel Patrick, Moira Lister, Michael Hordern

You Can't Beat the Irish (GB) Director: John Paddy Carstairs
Jack Warner, Barbara Mullen

1954 *Doctor in the House* (GB) (Betty Box) Director: Ralph Thomas
Dirk Bogarde, Kenneth More, James Robertson Justice

The Seekers (GB) aka *Land of Fury* (George Brown) Director:
Ken Annakin
Jack Hawkins, Glynis Johns, Kenneth Williams

Mad About Men (GB) (Betty Box) Director: Ralph Thomas
Glynis Johns, Donald Sinden, Margaret Rutherford

Svengali (GB) (Douglas Pierce) Director: Noel Langley
Donald Wolfit, Hildegarde Neff, Harry Secombe

1955 *Doctor at Sea* (GB) (Betty Box) Director: Ralph Thomas
Dirk Bogarde, Brigitte Bardot

1956 *Jacqueline* (GB) (George Brown) Director: Roy Baker
John Gregson, Jacqueline Ryan, Kathleen Ryan, Cyril Cusack

Lust for Life (USA) (MGM-John Houseman) Director Vincente
Minnelli
Kirk Douglas, Anthony Quinn

Moby Dick (GB) (Warner: John Huston) Director: John
Huston
Gregory Peck, Orson Welles, Richard Basehart

1957 *The Rising of the Moon*—Three Irish short stories (Ireland)
(Lord Killanin) Director: John Ford
"The Majesty of the Law" (Frank O'Connor)
Noel Purcell, Cyril Cusack

Doctor at Large (GB) (Betty Box) Director: Ralph Thomas
Dirk Bogarde, James Robertson Justice

1958 *Merry Andrew* (USA) (MGM-Sol C Siegel) Director: Michael
Kidd
Danny Kaye, Pier Angeli, Robert Coote

Ferry to Hong Kong (GB) (Geo Maynard) Director: Lewis
Gilbert
Curt Jurgens, Sylvia Syms, Orson Welles

Rockets Galore (GB) (Relph & Deardon) Director: Michael
Relph
Donald Sinden, Jeannie Carson, Ronald Culver

Rooney (GB) (George Brown) Director George Pollock
John Gregson, Barry Fitzgerald, Muriel Pavlow, Eddie Byrne

The Key (GB) (Columbia: Carl Foreman) Director: Carol
Reed
William Holden, Sophia Loren, Trevor Howard

1959 *Shake Hands with the Devil* (Ireland) (M Anderson) Director:
Michael Anderson
James Cagney, Glynis Johns, Michael Redgrave

Tommy the Toreador (GB) Director: John Paddy Carstairs
Tommy Steele, Janet Munro

The Three Worlds of Gulliver (US) (Charles Schneer) Director:
Jack Sher
Kerwin Mathews, Basil Sydney, June Thorburn, Jo Morrow

1960 *Man in the Moon* (GB) (Michael Ralph) Director: Basil
Dearden
Kenneth More, Shirley Anne Field, Michael Hordern

Watch Your Stern (GB) Director: Gerald Thomas
Kenneth Connor, Eric Barker

Make Mine Mink (GB) Director: Robert Asher
Terry Thomas, Athene Seyler, Billie Whitelaw

Carry on Cabby (GB) (Peter Rogers) Director: Gerald Thomas
Sid James, Kenneth Williams, Charles Hawtrey

Johnny Nobody (GB) (I Allen, A Broccoli) Director: Nigel
Patrick
Nigel Patrick, Aldo Ray, William Bendix, Jimmy O'Dea

The Millionairess (GB) (Dimitri de Grunwald) Director:
Anthony Asquith
Sophia Loren, Peter Sellers, Alastair Sim

1961 *Double Bunk* (GB) Director: CM Pennington-Richards
Ian Carmichael, Janette Scott

1962 *The Iron Maiden* (GB) (Peter Rogers) Director: Gerald Thomas
Michael Craig, Cecil Parker, Ronald Culver

Mutiny on the Bounty (USA) (MGM: Aaron Rosenberg)
Director: Lewis Milestone
Trevor Howard, Marlon Brando, Richard Harris

1963 *The Running Man* (GB) (Columbia: Carol Reed) Director
Carol Reed
Laurence Harvey, Alan Bates, Lee Remick

The List of Adrian Messenger (USA) (UI: Ed Lewis) Director: John Huston
George C Scott, Kirk Douglas, Clive Brook

Nurse on Wheels (GB) (Peter Rogers) Director: Gerald Thomas
Juliet Mills, Joan Sims, Raymond Huntley

The Ceremony (USA/Spain) (UA: Laurence Harvey) Director: Laurence Harvey
Laurence Harvey, Sarah Miles, Robert Walker

1964 *Lord Jim* (GB) (Columbia: Rene Dupont) Director: Richard Brooks
Peter O'Toole, James Mason, Eli Wallach

1965 *Doctor in Clover* (GB) aka *Carnaby MD* (Betty Box) Director: Ralph Thomas
Leslie Phillips, James Robertson Justice, Shirley Anne Field

1966 *Drop Dead Darling* (7 Arts: Ken Hughes) Director: Ken Hughes
Tony Curtis, Zsa Zsa Gabor, Nancy Kwan

1967 *I Spy, You Spy* (GB) Director: Don Sharp
Tony Randall, Senta Berger, Herbert Lom

1968 *Sinful Davey* (GB) (UA: W N Graf) Director: John Huston
John Hurt, Pamela Franklin, Robert Morley

The Violent Enemy (GB) (Wilfred Eades) Director: Don Sharp
Tom Bell, Ed Begley, Susan Hampshire

Where's Jack? (GB) (Paramount: Stanley Baker) Director:
James Clavell
Tommy Steele, Stanley Baker, Alan Badel

1970 *The McKenzie Break* (GB) (Warner: John Huston) Director:
John Huston
Brian Keith, Helmut Griem, Ian Hendry

1973 *The Mackintosh Man* (GB) (Warner: John Huston) Director:
John Huston
Paul Newman, James Mason, Dominique Sanda

In 1957 a film promoting the tourist attractions of Ireland called *Seven Wonders of Ireland* was sponsored by Bord Fáilte. Running length was thirty minutes and it was widely shown in the USA and Britain. Noel Purcell spoke the commentary.

DISCOGRAPHY

Glenside Records
Matrix No

	"The Dublin Saunter"	EPW 125
	"The Man Me Mother Married"	EPW 125
7xEP 193-1	"Kilcock"	EPW 142
7xEP 195-1	"Pretty Polly" (also on 78 rpm)	EPW 142
OEP 194	"What the Doctor Ordered"	W143
OEP 196	"McCarthy"	W143

EMI (Ireland) 1973

"The Filly with the Long Black Mane" EMD 4007A
"When I Was Young" EMD 4007B

Dolphin Records

"Brendan Behan" 145A
"The Rare Old Times" 145B

EMI (Ireland) 1977

12" LP Album Leaf 7016
(Also on Tape Cassette) Produced by Philip Greene
Folk Tales of Old Ireland
"The Well at the End of the World"

"Éadaoin—The Butterfly Girl"
"The Tale of Three Sisters"
"Brave Seán Rua"

Regal Zonophone (May 1933)
Car 2008-1 "The Last Drink"   MR1098
(With Jimmy O'Dea and Harry O'Donovan)

His Master's Voice (May 1938)
OEA 6632-1 "Fresh Fish"   MR 3109
(With Jimmy O'Dea and Harry O'Donovan)

Albums:

EMI (Ireland):
   Talisman (Transferred 1975)   STAL 1037
   Vol. One: Jimmy O'Dea and Harry O'Donovan
   Side Two: "Fresh Fish" (with Noel Purcell)

Compilation Albums

EMI (Ireland)—Stereo
   Memories of Dublin (Transferred 1984)
                                          STAL 8005
   Side Two: "Fresh Fish" with Jimmy O'Dea, Harry
   O'Donovan, Noel Purcell
   Side Two: "The Dublin Saunter" with Noel Purcell
   (With the bells of St Patrick's Cathedral, Dublin)

EMI (Ireland)
   The Golden Years of the Theatre Royal   GAR 1002
   Side One: "When I Was Young" with Noel Purcell

EMI (Ireland)

Jimmy O'Dea—the Pride of the Coombe
Tape Cassette. (Transferred 1990)   JOD MI
Side Two: "The Last Drink" with O'Dea, Harry
O'Donovan, Noel Purcell
Side Two: "Fresh Fish" with O'Dea, Harry O'Donovan,
Noel Purcell

MATERIAL IN RADIO ARCHIVES

RTE Radio Sound Archives

Accn No		Broadcast on:
S 04/77	Sports Items off acetates	
S 75/76	Noel and Eileen Purcell on Harry O'Donovan	
S AA3332	*Light of other days* (Noel Purcell)	06/10/67
S BBI133	*Speak your mind* (Noel Purcell)	10/11/71
S BBI20	Noel Purcell No 1 Talks to P Ó Raghallaigh	31/12/77
S BB121	Noel Purcell No 2 Talks to P Ó Raghallaigh	07/01/78
S BBI22	Noel Purcell No 3 Talks to P Ó Raghallaigh	14/01/78
S BBI23	Noel Purcell No 4 Talks to P Ó Raghallaigh	21/01/78
S BBI24	Noel Purcell No 5 Talks to P Ó Raghallaigh	28/01/78
S BB125	Noel Purcell No 6 Talks to P Ó Raghallaigh	04/02/78
S AAI224	*Reared on Tales and Stories* (Easter Prog.)	06/04/80
S AAI592	*Young at Heart* (Christmas Edition)	25/12/80
S AAI617	Leo Maguire, Walton's Documentary	03/01/81
S BB2941	Noel Purcell, 81st Birthday Party	23/12/81
S BB3245	*Appraisal*	07/03/85
S AA3093	*Balfe File*, Memories of Noel Purcell	10/03/85
S AA3806	*Spice of Life*—The Queen's Theatre	08/03/86
S AA3807	*Spice of Life*—Olympia and Capitol	15/03/86
S AA3809	*Spice of Life*—a Royal Occasion	29/03/86
S AA3814	*Spice of Life*—Noel Pearson Presents	03/05/86

| S AA3817 | *Spice of Life*—Final Curtain | 24/05/86 |
| S AA3997 | *Soundstage*—Variety Cavalcade | 14/08/88 |

Material Held in RTE VTR Library
Videotape Archives

Accn No   Relayed on

A GL011	No 11 Aga Khan Film Boxers (Gael-Linn)	21/08/59
A GLO13	No 13 Waterpolo Football (Gael-Linn)	04/09/59
A GLO43	No 43 Film Foal ICA Point to P (Gael-Linn)	01/04/60
A P88/62	Royal Years—Theatre Royal, Dublin	01/07/62
A GLI61	No 161 Theatre Zoo Judo Cork (Gael-Linn)	06/07/62
A P295/70	*Late Late*—Noel Purcell's Beard	01/01/70
A A60/810	*Late Late*—Noel Purcell Tribute (Tape 1 of 2)	22/12/73
A A60/803	*Late Late*—Noel Purcell Tribute (Tape 2 of 2)	22/12/73
A P282/74	*Féach*—21st Anniversary of Gael-Linn	14/10/74
A P375/74	*Going on 75*—People born in 1900	31/12/74
A 60/1002	*Peg o' My Heart* (Noel with Peggy Dell)	26/12/75
A P86/78	*Folio* (Mícheál Mac Liammóir Obituary)	09/03/78
A LB409	*Songs and Stories of Christmas*	25/12/79
A P599/80	*Raised on Song and Story* (Portrait of Noel)	24/12/80
A P29/81	*My Ireland* ("A Liberty Life": Tony Kenny)	09/01/81
A B90/1320	*Late Late Show* (Hal Roach)	26/11/83
A N180/84E	News Bulletin (Freedom of Dublin Conferred)	28/06/84
A P9/85	Remembering Jimmy O'Dea	07/01/85
A UN64/85D	Funeral of Noel Purcell (News Bulletin)	05/03/85

(The Gael-Linn newsreel material remains the copyright of Gael-Linn.)

STAGE APPEARANCES

Pantomimes

Jack the Giant Killer	(St Theresa's Hall, 1921)
Jack the Giant Killer	(Everyman Theatre, 1922–3)
Robinson Crusoe	(Queen's Theatre, 1928–9)
Little Red Riding Hood	(O'D Prod. Queen's Theatre, 1929–30)
Babes in the Wood	(O'D Prod. Olympia Theatre, 1930–1)
Dick Whittington	(O'D Prod. Olympia Theatre, 1931–2)
Cinderella	(O'D Prod. Olympia Theatre, 1932–3)
Mother Goose	(O'D Prod. Olympia Theatre, 1933–4)
Red Riding Hood	(O'D Prod. Olympia Theatre, 1934–5)
Jack and the Beanstalk	(O'D Prod. Olympia Theatre, 1935–6)
Ali Baba and the Forty Thieves	(O'D Prod. Olympia Theatre, 1936–7)
Mother Goose	(O'D Prod. Gaiety Theatre, 1937–8)
Cinderella	(O'D Prod. Gaiety Theatre, 1938–9)
Robinson Crusoe	(Queen's Theatre, 1939–40)
Mother Hubbard Goes to Town	(Theatre Royal, 1940–1)
Cinderella	(Theatre Royal, 1941–2)
Red Riding Hood	(Theatre Royal, 1942–3)
Puss in Boots	(Theatre Royal, 1943–4)
Mother Goose	(Theatre Royal, 1944–5)
Jack and the Beanstalk	(Theatre Royal, 1945–6)
Babes in the Wood	(Gaiety Theatre, 1946–7)

Robinson Crusoe	(Theatre Royal, 1951–2)
Babes in the Wood	(Theatre Royal, 1952–3)
Mother Goose	(Theatre Royal, 1955–6)

Plays

Bunty Pulls the Strings	(Gaiety, 1914)
The Brass Bottle	(Gaiety, 1914)
A Phoenix on the Roof	(Hardwicke Hall, 1915)
Juno and the Paycock	(Gaiety, 1941)
Red Roses for Me	(Gaiety, 1946)
The Shadow of a Gunman	(Gaiety, 1946)
The Silver Tassie	(Gaiety, 1947)
Paul Twyning	(Gaiety, 1947)
The End of the Beginning	(Gaiety, 1947)
The Devil Came from Dublin	(Olympia, 1955)
The Samson Riddle [Reading]	(Gate Theatre, 1972)

Revues

Tom Powell's *Revue* (Olympia Theatre, 1928)

Irish Smiles

(O'D Prod. Irish and English tour; Coliseum Theatre London, 1930)

O'D Prod. *Revues* (Irish and British Tours, 1930–9)

Gaiety Revels (O'D Prod. Gaiety Theatre, 1937;1938;1940)

Anything May Happen (NP Prod. Empire Theatre, Belfast, 1940)

Hullabaloo (Theatre Royal, 1941)

That's That! (Queen's Theatre, 1942)

Something in the Air (Theatre Royal, 1943) (Series)

Variety Fair and Royal Bouquet (Theatre Royal, 1944) (Series)

Royal Review (Theatre Royal, 1945) (Series)

Royal Spotlight (Theatre Royal, 1946) (Series)

Other Theatre Royal Shows

Royal Flush; Royal Parade; Confetti (1945); *Cheerio; See-Saw; Cap and Bells* (Series)

Short Original Musicals at Theatre Royal

Trouble in Troy; Castles in Spain; Frolics in Spring   (One week each)

...And Pastures New (Gaiety Theatre, 1946)

Many Happy Returns (Theatre Royal, 1947)

Easter Cavalcade (Theatre Royal, 1949)

High Times (Theatre Royal, 1951) (Series)

Royal Travelcade (Theatre Royal, 1953) (Series)

Royal Finale (Theatre Royal, 1962) (Final Night)

Miscellaneous

HMS Pinafore (Gaiety Theatre, 1914)

You Ain't Heard Nuthin' Yet (Gaiety Theatre, 1976)

Cinderella's Christmas Dream (Goff's, 1976)

Joseph and the Amazing Technicolor Dreamcoat (Gaiety Theatre, 1978)

Tosca (Cameo Appearances, Gaiety Theatre, 1962, 1982)

Night of 100 Stars (Gaiety Theatre, 1984)

BIBLIOGRAPHY

Ellman, Richard. *James Joyce*. Oxford University Press, 1966.

Green, Benny (Ed). *The Last Empires*. London: Pavilion Books Ltd, 1986.

Billington, Michael. *Theatre Facts and Feats*. London: Guinness Superlatives Ltd (1982).

Freeney, William J. *Drama in Hardwicke Street*. London and Toronto: Associated University Press, 1984.

MacInnes, Colin. *Sweet Saturday Night*. London: MacGibbon and Kee, 1967.

INDEX